A POCKET GUIDE

CELTIC WALES

A POCKET GUIDE

CELTIC WALES

MIRANDA GREEN and RAY HOWELL

CARDIFF
UNIVERSITY OF WALES PRESS
THE WESTERN MAIL
2000

Published by the University of Wales Press and The Western Mail.

British Library Cataloguing in Publication Data
A catalogue record for this book is available from the British Library

ISBN 0-7083-1532-1

Front cover: Part of an enamelled bronze bowl-handle in the form of a cat's face from Snowdon, Gwynedd (by permission of the National Museums and Galleries of Wales). Photograph of Dinas Emrys (in foreground) and Snowdon © Mick Sharp Photography.

Cover design by Chris Neale
Typeset by the University of Wales Press
Printed in Great Britain by Dinefwr Press, Llandybïe

Contents

Acknowledgements

The authors would like to express their gratitude to the staff of the Department of Archaeology and Numismatics, The National Museums & Galleries of Wales for their help in preparing the publication. They are also grateful to the University of Wales College, Newport for its support in the project, and to the staff of the University of Wales Press for their professionalism and encouragement.

MJAG and RH

The authors and publishers wish to thank the copyright holders who have kindly permitted the reproduction of photographs as follows:

Korisios sword-stamp (p. 5) by permission of Bernisches Historisches Museum, Bern.

Celtic village (p. 14) by permission of the National Museums & Galleries of Wales (Museum of Welsh Life).

Druids on Anglesey (p. 34) from *Druidism, the Ancient Faith of Britain* by Dudley Wright (Thames and Hudson).

Trawsfynydd tankard (p. 30) by permission of the National Museums & Galleries on Merseyside.

Basilica, Caerwent (p. 54), Caerwent temple reconstruction (p. 67), Degannwy Castle (p. 91), Maen Achwyfan cross-slab (p. 97), by permission of Cadw: Welsh Historic Monuments. Crown Copyright.

Llantwit Major villa (p. 57), copyright of G. de la Bedoyère.

Vortipor (p. 88), from *Early Christian Monuments of Wales* by V. E. Nash-Williams (University of Wales Press).

Epona (p. 105), in the collection of Rheinisches Landesmuseum Bonn. Photograph: Miranda Green.

Bronze plaque (p. 39), Silurian warrior (p. 46), samian bowl (p. 73), Magnus Maximus coin (p. 78), bronze cauldron (p. 113), wrought iron fire dog (colour section p. 1), crescentric bronze plaque (colour section p. 4), painting of Llyn Fawr (colour section p. 2), Snowdon cat's face bowl-handle (colour section p. 4), plaque from Moel Hiraddug (colour section p. 1), Dinorben bull-head (colour section p. 5), Dinas Powys brooch (colour section p. 6), Hywel ap Rhys cross (colour section p. 7), by permission of the National Museums & Galleries of Wales.

Caerwent mother goddess (colour section p. 5), by permission of Newport Museum and Art Gallery.

Gower boar (colour section p. 8), by permission of the Ashmolean Museum, Oxford.

Zürich gold bowl (colour section p. 8), by permission of the Swiss National Museum.

Lindow moss bog-body (colour section p. 3), Dolaucothi gold necklace (colour section p. 6) © the British Museum.

To

Stephen, Jadwiga,

Elisabeth and David

Preface

This book has come about because of a perceived need for a concise, yet scholarly and up-to-date account of Wales during the Iron Age, Roman and early medieval periods. The authors teach a successful MA course in 'Celto-Roman Studies', and they have written *A Pocket Guide: Celtic Wales* with both students and the informed general reader in mind.

The decision has been taken to use the 1974–96 county names as far as possible, but to retain Anglesey, on the one hand, and to unify Glamorgan, on the other. The reason for this choice is that these boundaries are both geographically and historically appropriate and serve to define regions that remain meaningful today.

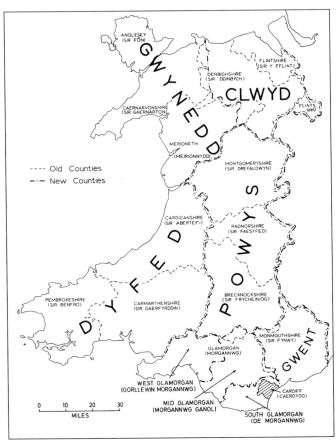

The main administrative units of Wales, before and after local government reorganization in 1974.

Prelude

Wales did not exist as an entity in prehistoric or Roman times. Indeed, the region of the British Isles that we now call Wales did not become 'Welsh' until Roman influence declined, a language recognizable as Welsh emerged and small kingdoms were formed. This book sets out to explore the evidence for British settlement and society in the area which coincides with the boundaries of modern Wales during the period from later prehistory (from *c.* 700 BC) to the tenth century AD. This long span of some fifteen centuries covers a period of time which has long been labelled as 'Celtic', a term first adopted by Classical writers in the sixth century BC, to identify and describe communities living in much of temperate Europe, which these observers considered as being different from their own and yet which possessed sufficient homogeneity to allow the application of a single name. The terms 'Celts' and 'Celtic' are the subject of lively current debate. In our opinion, the term 'Celtic' has the same sort of validity as today's use of 'European', encompassing linkages between groups of people while recognizing regional diversity. Certain features of material culture, notably styles of art, demonstrate some commonality within Europe, and the highly symbolic nature of this art makes it more than likely that the people making and using it possessed some shared 'mindset' which enabled its 'currency' throughout the huge region between Ireland and Hungary. Moreover, early linguistic evidence clearly demonstrates linkages over this area and beyond, into Asia Minor (Galatia).

The book begins with a brief synopsis of Celtic Wales in its wider geographical context, together with an analysis of current issues, such as the nature of 'Celticity' (chapter 1). There follows a survey of the early Iron Age in Wales (chapter 2), when the only evidence at our disposal is the archaeological record. Important sites of this period include the fortified hill settlements, or 'hillforts', of Llanmelin, Tre'r Ceiri, Twyn y Gaer and Moel y Gaer, to name but a few, and the lacustrine sites of Llyn Fawr and Llyn Cerrig Bach, both foci for the ritual deposit of votive offerings. The evidence for technology, trade and economy is examined, and the chapter ends with a brief account of the splendid legacy of Celtic art, as reflected in such prestigious decorated metalwork as the Capel Garmon fire-dog and the Tal-y-llyn plaques. It is noteworthy that Celtic art did not wither and die under Roman influence but re-emerged to decorate stone crosses and illuminated manuscripts in the early Christian period. Investigation of the Iron Age in Wales reveals enormous gaps in our knowledge and understanding of the pre-Roman period in the last 300 years BC.

Chapter 3 investigates the nature of the interaction between the Britons in Wales and the Romans. The Roman forces found it difficult to subdue the Welsh tribes. The intensity of military resistance, particularly by the Ordovices in the north and the Silures in the south, coupled with the very difficult, mountainous terrain (ideal for guerrilla warfare) over much of the region, led to bloody conflict that, according to the writings of the Roman political historian Tacitus, lasted until AD 77, when his father-in-law, Gnaeus Julius Agricola, finally pacified the north. This chapter also explores the Roman occupation of Wales, the literary testimony to the military campaigns and the resistance of the Welsh tribes. Although, from the mid-first century AD, we possess written chronicles from Roman historians such as Tacitus, we still have to rely upon archaeology to gain a detailed picture of the Roman period in Wales. Archaeological evidence can help to answer questions about the nature and dating of Roman military installations: marching-camps, auxiliary forts and legionary fortresses. It enables us to pose questions about the different regional character of romanization (or cultural interaction) in north and south Wales, the nature of urban and rural settlement, religion and ritual. It is archaeological exploration of Roman sites in Wales that puts flesh on the bare bones of written testimony. Excavations at the Silurian *civitas* capital at Caerwent in the 1980s and 1990s have yielded a great deal of new information about life in a Romano-British town. Likewise, modern investigation of such important military sites as Usk, Caerleon and Segontium serve to demonstrate the complexity of the Roman military presence, the disposition of forces, troop movements and fort-networks. Study of rural settlement reveals a wide variety of communities living outside the towns, from the highly sophisticated Roman villas of the Vale of Glamorgan – like Llantwit Major – to much humbler dwellings, such as Thornwell Farm, Chepstow and Bryn Eryr on Anglesey, which show little sign of *romanitas*. What is very striking is the extent of continuity of settlement from the Iron Age to the Roman period.

By the end of the fourth century, even in those areas where *romanitas* can be demonstrated by evidence from sites such as villas and towns, significant changes were apparent; and chapter 4 looks at the transition in Wales from paganism to Christianity, and the decline of *romanitas*. Some of the changes which took place during this early post-Roman period, such as the emergence of Christianity, were firmly rooted in the late Roman tradition. There is good evidence to confirm that the first Christians in Wales were early converts. Three Romano-British martyrs, Alban, Julius and Aaron, are known and the latter two of these died in Wales. From AD 313 and Constantine's 'Peace of the Church', Christianity enjoyed legal protection in the Roman Empire. When, in the following year, the Council of Arles was called, three British bishops attended, confirming that the insular church was already well established.

As Roman political control declined, new political and social structures emerged. These changes, which shaped sub-Roman and early medieval Wales (chapter 5), are best explored archaeologically and interesting clues are provided by sites such as Dinas Emrys, Degannwy and Dinorben. An especially important early medieval site is Dinas Powys, an apparently high-status secular site with evidence of both local industrial activity and very wide-ranging trade connections. Excavations during the 1970s at nearby Llandough have confirmed the presence of an important ecclesiastical foundation and examination of evidence from both these sites may significantly enhance our understanding of post-Roman Wales.

One of the most interesting questions about early medieval developments is the extent to which survivals of 'native tradition' can be demonstrated. In some cases, it is possible to argue that aspects of culture show clear links to pre-Roman peoples. The investigation of these connections and the extent to which it is possible to speak in terms of 'Celtic continuity' is an important theme in this book. The early Welsh kingdoms matured and social structures developed, although – once again – external influences were strong and, at times, threatening. The cultural synthesis that emerges in Wales represents another important theme of this volume.

The final section in the book (chapter 6) is concerned with the earliest medieval mythic tradition. The first mythological Welsh narratives consist of the *Pedeir Keinc y Mabinogi* and *Culhwch ac Olwen*, which were compiled in written form no earlier than the

3

thirteenth century AD. However, many scholars believe that such mythic tales contain resonances of a far earlier and pagan past, and it is certainly possible to identify specific features of correspondence between this body of Welsh texts and the archaeological and iconographic evidence for pre-Christian Celtic Europe. Particular themes explored here include triplism, the veneration of the human head, shape-shifting and the prominence of animals, sacred cauldrons, the treatment of female and male characters and the interface between paganism and Christianity. The question of whether discernible resonances (or apparent relationships) between late prehistoric and early historical pasts, in terms of genuine linkages, have any validity is raised. Is the relationship between archaeology and myth connection or coincidence?

The region we now know as Wales has had an exciting and dynamic early history. The period chosen as the subject for this book is perhaps the most interesting and challenging of all, depending as it does upon a subtle interplay between material culture and documentary sources, each of which presents its own opportunities and problems. Given the constraints of length, such a book can act only as a tantalizing introduction to a rich, complex phase of Wales's past, in a fascinating region situated – in antiquity at least – towards the edge of the known world. We hope that the further reading section at the end of the volume will take the reader further along the journey of discovery.

1 Celtic Wales in its European Context

Questions of 'Celticity'

It is inevitable that a book entitled *Celtic Wales* has to engage with the question of whether or not it is justifiable to use the term 'Celts' to describe certain ancient European communities. This problem is the subject of much lively current debate in academia, particularly among scholars of European Iron Age archaeology. Some prehistorians argue that it is invalid to conflate evidence for material culture, the comments of Classical observers on their 'barbarian' neighbours and early linguistic evidence to create a 'Celtic' past. However, it is occasionally possible to bring together language and material culture: a prime example of how this can happen is the discovery of a 'typical' La Tène sword from Port in Switzerland, which bears its maker's Celtic name KORISIOS stamped on it.

Sword-stamp from an iron La Tène sword, from Port in Switzerland: first century BC. The maker's name 'Korisios', written in Greek characters, is Celtic. This is a good example of the convergence between material culture and language at the end of European prehistory.

Romancing the Celts

The 'myths of Celticity' have been nourished by the early modern romanticism that has so heavily overlain the concept of 'Celts', with its largely spurious notions of continuity from remote antiquity to the present. Such constructions are well illustrated by the activities of Iolo Morganwg who, in the late eighteenth and early nineteenth century, created a 'pedigree' of Celtic Welsh bardism stretching from his day back to pre-Roman times, and by the eighteenth-century antiquarian William Stukeley who, in his later years, saw himself as the reincarnation of a mythical ancient Gaulish druid, Chyndonax.

The polarization of current opinion on Celticity is exemplified by the views of John Collis and Simon James, on the one hand, who vigorously challenge the validity of the term 'Celtic' as a means of labelling the later prehistoric European past, and of Vincent and Ruth Megaw and Barry Cunliffe, on the other, who argue in favour of 'Celts' and 'Celtic' as useful descriptors for a loosely knit but, in some ways, coherent group of ancient communities. Those opposed to this use of 'Celtic' argue their case on several fronts. They claim that the concept of Celticity is largely a construct of the early modern period in western Europe; they also protest that, as an ethnic label, the term 'Celtic' has the potential to be hijacked as a means of exclusive, separatist and, ultimately, dangerously nationalistic political determination. They also see it as imposing a misleading homogeneity on a diverse range of Iron Age cultures, and, moreover, they correctly point out that the use of the 'Celtic' label for ancient Britain is particularly problematical since it was never so used in antiquity. Caesar, for example, spoke of *Britanni*, not *Galli* or *Celtae* for the inhabitants of Britain in the mid-first century BC, although he also admits to the close connections between Gaul and at least the south-east of Britain.

Those in favour of using 'Celtic' for the classification of material culture argue that it is a term employed widely by ancient writers (such as Herodotus, Caesar, Polybius, Pausanias and Strabo) to describe the peoples of Gaul and Central Europe. In addition, pro-Celticists perceive the presence of sufficient commonality in aspects of Iron Age European material culture – art is perhaps the best example – to justify the use of a single identifier for this final phase of European prehistory. Furthermore, these recurrent elements in material culture seem to correlate geographically – to an extent – with evidence (from place-names, for instance) for the distribution of Celtic languages. The pro-Celtic scholars would not, for one moment, attempt to equate the Celtic labelling of archaeological communities with acknowledgements of ethnicity: such an equation would, indeed, be totally unjustifiable; ethnicity is a special problem which it is, arguably, impossible to verify by archaeological means. Followers of Celtic studies are acutely aware that groups of disparate evidence – language, material culture and the testimony of Classical writers – are not coterminous and must never be treated as though they are.

The position of the present authors on Celticity is somewhat of a middle way between two extremes. We fully accept that there are dangers is using a single term to label a chronologically and culturally diverse set of communities living in Europe at the time of the Roman conquest, and for half a millennium beforehand. Huge diversities between regions were clearly present: within Britain alone, during the first millennium BC, considerable differences in material culture between – say – Wales and south-eastern England and, indeed, between north, west and south Wales can be discerned. On the other hand, it is impossible to ignore or deny the existence of recurrent idiosyncracies of material culture that present themselves over huge areas of temperate Iron Age Europe. These 'markers' of commonality include coins, torcs (neckrings), the prominence given to the human head (in terms of both ritual treatment and imagery), the aquatic deposition of prestigious – frequently martial – objects and, above all, motifs in (La Tène) art, mainly on metalwork, including such elements – repeated over time and space – as leaf-crowns, triskeles, yin-yangs, fantastic animals and human heads. Such common features of material culture must be explicable in terms of close relationships, of whatever kind, between large tracts of Europe. Moreover, many of these 'markers' continue to feature during and after the Roman occupation, suggesting that the links survived this cultural disruption imposed by Roman imperial colonialism.

One crucial issue which, as mentioned briefly above, it is impossible to resolve is the question of self-determination. How far, if at all, did 'Celts' recognize themselves as part of a wide network of cognate communities and who, if anybody, identified themselves as Celts in the ancient world? Since the Iron Age communities in question were, to all intents and purposes, non-literate, we cannot gain insight into their self-identification. All we have is the literature of contemporary observers from the Mediterranean world, who identified certain peoples living to their north and west as *Keltoi*, *Celtae*, *Galli* or *Galatae* and – in Britain – as *Britanni*. So we cannot know to what extent these labels were simply external impositions or were meaningful to these people themselves. We do not encounter the same problem with the Greeks and Romans since authors belonging to Greece and Rome clearly so identify themselves and their fellow citizens. However, in voicing difficulties about using such a blanket term as 'Celtic' to describe divergent communities, it should be remembered that Herodotus, in the fifth century BC, used the term 'Greek' (as do Classicists today) of vigorously independent city-states whose citizens (despite a common language) thought of themselves primarily as Athenians, Spartans or Corinthians rather than as Greeks. Similarly, there seems no difficulty about using the cultural label 'Roman' to identify peoples living in regions as widely separated as Spain and the Rhineland, Britain and North Africa, despite obvious cultural differences. The generic term 'Celtic' might be equally valid to describe divergent groups with certain characteristics in common, particularly if they shared sufficient cultural features to cause their Mediterranean neighbours to bestow on them a common identifier.

Avoidance of the term 'Celtic' to describe Iron Age European communities – despite the problems of its use – causes its own difficulties which can be seen as at least as serious. Perhaps the most obvious stumbling-block lies in finding an alternative. Opponents of 'Celticism' might argue that no alternative is needed, but that answer is not, to our minds, satisfactory. Certain scholars favour the term 'barbarian Europe' to describe communities beyond the Mediterranean littoral. We would protest that such a term is, at best, meaningless and, at worst, unacceptably pejorative. Others suggest using the term 'La Tène', since the Swiss Iron Age lake-shore site has given its name to a distinctive group of artefacts and art-styles found widely within temperate Europe from the fifth century BC to the Roman conquest and beyond. But this label is equally problematical, both because it is a totally artificial, modern, label and because it can only accurately describe discrete forms of metalwork and art which are by no means universally distributed. Despite its problems, the use of the term 'Celtic' at least has the advantage of being an ancient term used by literate peoples of antiquity to describe their con-

Celticity and language

It is language, above all, that has led to the construction of linkages between the Celts of antiquity and the Celtic-speaking areas of modern Europe. There is a sense in which such a claim has some validity, inasmuch as a range of scattered inscriptions written in ancient languages that are unequivocally Celtic, and dating as early as the fourth century BC, are recorded from Iberia, Gaul, North Italy and Galatia (part of modern Turkey). Such epigraphic evidence clearly demonstrates the presence of a wide range of Celtic speakers in antiquity.

It was a Welshman, Edward Lhuyd who, in his *Archaeologia Britannica* of 1709 and his fellow linguist Paul-Yves Pezron in 1703, in his *Antiquité de la nation, et de langue des Celtes, autrement appellés Gaulois*, who put forward the notion of shared Celtic linguistic (and ethnic) identity among the non-English Britons, Irish and Bretons, and grouped what is undoubtedly a family of related languages under the 'Celtic' umbrella. What is problematical is any attempt at making direct and precise correlations between the material culture of Iron Age Europe, the Celtic-speaking regions of the past and the present-day Celtic countries or regions. If the term 'Celtic' is admissible as a label for European antiquity, then it is clearly a different 'Celtic' from that used to identify languages. The linguistic term 'Celtic' – which describes the cognate languages of Welsh, Scots Gaelic, Irish, Breton, Cornish and Manx – must, therefore, not be confused either with the archaeological evidence for shared traits in Iron Age European material culture or with the ethnic identification of ancient Celts by writers of the Classical world. One reason why the anti-Celt lobby is so vociferous is that such confusion and conflation has taken place all too regularly, in a manner which is academically unacceptable.

temporary neighbours. Caesar begins his *De Bello Gallico* by commenting of the peoples of *Gallia Comata*, 'All Gaul is divided into three parts, one of which the Belgae inhabit, the Aquitani another, those who in their own language are called Celts, in ours Gauls, the third'. Purists would argue that – *sensu stricto* – the term 'Celts' should, therefore, only be used to identify people living in central Gaul, but Caesar is not our only literary source for the term, and other ancient writers use it much less specifically. We would argue that, as long as the Celtic nomenclature is specifically and precisely defined, it remains a convenient descriptor for certain past communities living north of the Classical world, even if it is as modern and artificial as 'Bronze Age' or 'Iron Age'.

Finally, we have to take cognizance of present-day Celtic self-identification. Even supposing that the archaeological Celts were to be nothing more than a label imposed on the past by modern archaeo-historians, it is none the less the case that today Celtic self-identification is very real for millions of people living on the western periphery of Europe (in Cornwall, Wales, Ireland, Scotland, the Isle of Man, Brittany and Galícia). However spurious or mythical the foundations of 'Celts' and 'Celticity', it is necessary to be aware that latter-day Celts have a strong sense of unity, not only in terms of language but also in music, literature and independence from the powerful nation states of England, France and Spain.

Geography, chronology and culture

In attempting to identify a remote 'Celtic' past, it is necessary to consider the evidence from archaeology, linguistics and contemporary literature. Even when combined, these three sources of information can do no more than produce a fragmentary, elusive and distorted picture and one which has to be regarded with a degree of scepticism.

In terms of the archaeological evidence, the emergence of a Celtic material culture in temperate Europe coincides – broadly speaking – with the introduction of iron technology and the use of iron for functional objects (particularly those requiring a hard edge), such as swords, spears and knives. The Continental Iron Age has been divided by archaeologists into two main phases, each named after a 'type-site' (a findspot for a large assemblage of diagnostically distinctive material). The first phase, the Hallstatt Iron Age (*c.* 750–500 BC), derives its title from a small lakeside village in Austria, which was the centre of a thriving salt-mining industry during the first millennium BC. Here, at Hallstatt, a huge cemetery has been excavated, containing a wide variety of grave-goods, including pottery, weapons and jewellery. The archaeological classificatory labels for the Hallstatt period follow the chronology of the cemetery, which spans the later Bronze Age (Hallstatt A and B) and the earlier Iron Age (Hallstatt C and D). Although very little true Continental Hallstatt material has been found in Britain, the Welsh site of Llyn Fawr, with its Hallstatt C-type iron sword together with other exotic metalwork (see chapter 2) of the period from the eighth–seventh century BC, has produced some of the earliest Iron Age artefacts from Britain.

We know most about the Hallstatt Iron Age from the Continental graves of the wealthy élite, who made their fortunes from salt-trading and the control of other mineral resources such as copper and tin. Some tombs, particularly in Baden-Württemberg, southern Germany, comprised great mounds covering wooden mortuary enclosures containing the inhumed bodies of the deceased. Tomb-furniture might include a four-wheeled wagon or hearse on which the body was conveyed to the grave, together with all the paraphernalia the dead person might require in the afterlife.

The golden chieftain

One especially lavish burial, from Hochdorf, near Stuttgart (dated to c. 530 BC) contained the body of a 'chieftain', about forty years old, lying on a splendidly ornamental bronze couch, and equipped with archery and fishing equipment, a gold-decorated dagger, gold jewellery and even gold-embellished shoes. At his feet was a large sheet-bronze cauldron, imported from the Greek world, that had been filled with 400 litres of a honey-based liquor; hanging on the walls of the tomb-chamber were nine drinking-horns and on the wheeled bier was a nine-piece dinner service.

The tombs of the wealthy demonstrate that the élite were essentially a warrior-aristocracy, for whom trading, riding, fighting and feasting were favoured occupations. The contents of these graves are also testimony to close trading (or gift-exchange) links with the Classical world. That women, as well as men, could enjoy high rank is shown, for instance, by the grave-mound at Hohmichele in Germany, where a couple were interred side by side, each furnished with rich grave-goods, including Chinese silk. Another rich Hallstatt burial, at Vix in Burgundy, has long been accepted as that of a woman, although some scholars are now questioning the gender-identity of the body entombed there. If it is a female grave, it is of particular interest because the Vix burial may be that of the chief who ruled at the nearby stronghold of Mont Lassois. A number of fortified high-status centres, or hillforts, of this period are known, perhaps the best documented being the Heuneberg in Germany. But knowledge of the settlements inhabited by ordinary people is sadly deficient, although the well-preserved organic remains of wood-built 'lake-villages' are recorded, for example at the Federsee in Germany.

La Tène metalwork has been identified over a very broad sweep of Europe: from Ireland to the Carpathians and from Scotland to Italy. Apart from specific weapon-types, the most striking characteristic is an idiosyncratic, highly distinctive art, decorating functional and ornamental objects (primarily but by no means solely of metal) which, although derived ultimately from vegetal, faunal and anthropomorphic themes, and despite undoubted inspiration from the Classical world, was driven by an individualistic and innovative delight in schematism, abstraction, ambiguity and fantasy. Thus, horned, bulbous-eyed human faces peer from sinuously curving tendrils; animals are transformed into monsters; realism merges with design to produce triskeles with birds' heads

Pilgrimage to La Tène

The second phase of the Continental Iron Age has been known, since 1874, as 'La Tène', after the type-site of that name, on the shore of Lake Neuchâtel, near Thun in Switzerland. The site was discovered in 1857, when the water level in the lake dropped and revealed a series of wooden structures. Upon investigation over several decades, the mud of the lake-bed was found to conceal a rich assemblage of weapons, tools and jewellery, spanning a period from the fifth–first centuries BC, together with wooden objects, animal bones and human remains. Opinion is divided as to why this material accumulated at La Tène over this long timespan: it may have been a settlement or a place of ritual pilgrimage, where people recurrently made offerings – including, perhaps, human sacrifice – to the gods of the lake.

and seemingly abstract patterns resolve themselves into cartoon faces.

On the Continent, La Tène art had tailed off by the first century BC but, in Britain, many of the most technically brilliant pieces belong to the first centuries BC and AD. In regions on the peripheries – Wales and northern Britain – La Tène-derived art was still being actively produced in the second century AD and, in Ireland, never conquered by the Romans, the La Tène of the pagan period became the foundation for a new flowering of manuscript-art in the early medieval Christian period. Thus, the ninth-century Book of Kells is decorated with motifs and symbols, such as triskeles, which can be traced back at least as early as the fifth century BC.

Commonality and diversity

La Tène metalwork formed only a part of a distinctive 'package' of material culture that possessed considerable regional and chronological diversity. A striking aspect of this archaeological evidence, once again, comes from tombs: in some regions, notably in the Marne area of eastern France, élite burials were characterized by the interment of some individuals with light two-wheeled carts (or chariots), occasionally accompanied by the horses that had drawn them. The graves at La Gorge Meillet and Somme-Bionne in France typify this tradition. Cart-burial took place in Britain, too, being clustered in east Yorkshire: here both men's and women's graves were furnished with these high-status vehicles. But methods of British and Continental body-disposal varied greatly, both spatially and temporally. During the first centuries BC and AD, a distinctive type of prestige burial rite, occurring in certain areas, consisted of the cremation of people with elaborate feasting equipment, including jars of wine and olive oil from the Mediterranean world, together with locally made, bronze-bound buckets, sheet-bronze cauldrons and pottery. Such graves are exemplified by those belonging to Treveran noblemen at Göblingen-Nospelt in Luxembourg and to high-ranking Catuvellaunians at Welwyn in south-east England. But despite the prominence of graves like these and the earlier cart-burials, the great majority of the Iron Age population, particularly in Britain, was apparently accorded no formal funerary rites that have survived in the archaeological record; indeed many people's bodies may have been subjected to excarnation (exposure until the flesh decayed) and their bones scattered.

In terms of settlement, in the La Tène phase of the European Iron Age, people lived in various configurations of community, both urban and rural. Some inhabited large, well-fortified communal hillforts, like Maiden Castle in southern England and Bibracte in Burgundy; others in small 'villages', like Gussage All Saints in Dorset; others again in individual families farming small-holdings, like Little Woodbury in Wiltshire. There was considerable regional variety of dwelling: only in Scotland, for instance, are the idiosyncratic stone tower-houses, or 'brochs' known. In Ireland, large and so-called 'royal sites', like Emhain Macha in Co. Armagh and Tara in Co. Meath are unparalleled elsewhere. In the

Reconstructed Iron Age roundhouses at the 'Celtic Village', Museum of Welsh Life, Saint Fagan's (Cardiff). The architecture of the houses is informed by the remains of various structures excavated on Iron Age British sites, including Moel y Gaer. Houses like these range in diameter from 7 to 11m.

later Iron Age, very large proto-towns, or *oppida* (a term used by Caesar in his *De Bello Gallico*), often in lowland areas, are exemplified by Manching, which controlled traffic along and across the Danube in Bavaria, Guignicourt in the Aisne Valley of France, and Camulodunum (modern-day Colchester) in south-east England. Communal settlements like these were true urban centres, with centralized organization and production of commodities, large-scale import and export and coin-minting.

Literary evidence

There exists a solid body of references to *Keltoi, Celtae, Galli* or *Galatae* from Classical literature, from the fifth century BC to the fourth century AD. Two early Greek writers who allude to Celts are Hecataeus of Miletus and Herodotus, both of whom make statements concerning their geographical position: Hecataeus speaks of Celts living in both southern Gaul and in the eastern Alpine region; Herodotus places the Danube in Celtic territory. We learn from Classical chroniclers that the *Galli* invaded Italy in the early fourth century BC and overran the Greek sanctuary of Delphi in 279; during the third century BC, some Celts established settlements in Asia Minor (Saint Paul's Galatians). Earlier than this, Celts were fighting as mercenaries in the fourth century, employed by the Spartans against their fellow Peloponnesian city-state of Thebes. Polybius and Livy give accounts of Celtic incursions into Italy in the fourth and third centuries BC; in 218 BC, Hannibal used Celtic mercenaries against the Romans in Italy during the Carthaginian wars. Although the Celts sustained a crushing defeat at the Battle of Telamon in 225 BC, Celtic tribes, such as the Boii, settled permanently in northern Italy. Writers such as the first-century BC geographer Strabo describe the Celtic presence in Iberia, some of whom – presumably an ethnic mixture of Celts and indigenous Iberians – were known as Celtiberians. Poseidonios, Caesar, Livy and others provide detailed information on the Celts of Gaul. Caesar was the first Roman to present useful comments on Britain and, whilst he does not call the Britons Celts, he does allude to close linkages between Gaul and the tribes of south-eastern Britain. For Britain during the Roman conquest in the first century AD, Tacitus is our most reliable source; he describes British tribes not only in southern England but also in Wales and northern Britain.

Early linguistic evidence

The evidence for the spread and distribution of Celtic languages is inevitably extremely sparse, given the virtual absence of literacy in temperate Europe before the Roman occupation. Early Celtic languages are recorded on a few inscriptions from Spain, France and Italy, and on coin-legends (see p. 9). Pre-Roman inscriptions can sometimes be very informative: one incised on a lead sheet from Larzac in southern Gaul records the existence of two guilds of female magicians. Additionally, place-names identifiable as of Celtic origin are recorded by Classical writers and on inscriptions of Roman date. The word *nemeton* (meaning 'sacred place') is very widely distributed from Britain (for example Aquae Arnemetiae – Buxton) and Gaul (for example Nemetocenna) to Galatia in Asia Minor (Drunemeton). A Gallo-Roman goddess worshipped among the Treveri of the Moselle Valley was Nemetona; she is also recorded as having followers at Bath in western Britain. Likewise, words incorporating such elements as *briga* (Brigantia in Britain, Conimbriga in Portugal) and *dunum* (Camulodunum in Britain, Noviodunum in Gaul, for example) occur over large areas of Europe.

Conclusion

Supporters of the perception of an ancient Celtic Europe, stretching – at its apogée – from Britain to the Carpathians and Asia Minor and from Spain to Austria, can point to a combination of archaeological evidence (particularly La Tène metalwork), linguistic indicators and the observations of contemporary writers from the Greek and Roman world as ammunition for their cause. Opponents of such a unified scenario can just as persuasively claim that the Classical literature is not necessarily to be relied upon and that diversity of material culture within temperate Europe is testimony to much greater fragmentation than linkage between communities. Ultimately, the problem is incapable of resolution. Material culture, language and historical reporting are all ambiguous indicators of identity. People can adopt the material culture of foreign neighbours without being ethnically linked, although they may be. For example, drinking Coca Cola and wearing Levi jeans does not make one an American, nor does drinking Burgundy make one French. Communities may speak one of a family of interrelated languages without perceiving themselves as sharing identity; English-speaking Indians, for example, do not regard themselves as anything other than Indian. The Classical authors who wrote about their northern neighbours were foreign observers, commenting on cultures alien, and often, perhaps, incomprehensible, to them. Moreover, they were not so much concerned with accuracy in ethnic determination as in noting the 'otherness' of non-Mediterranean communities. One Graeco-Roman author and another may have used the term 'Celt' and 'Celtic' in completely different senses one from the other. Were Caesar's Celts the same as those of Herodotus? Were Polybius and Hecataeus speaking of the same cultural phenomenon?

Whatever the nature of linkage or disconnection between ancient Europeans of the later first millennium BC, some cultural elements were undeniably shared, whether by virtue of trade, the presence of peripatetic craftsmen sharing and introducing artistic traditions, gradual cultural accretion or actual folk movement. The presence of recurrent symbolism within the La Tène artistic tradition over large areas of Europe is highly significant in this respect, since it implies a shared currency of meaning: in other words, it might be tenable to assume that the torc or the triskele, for example, conveyed a common symbolic message within a La Tène context whether they occurred in Britain or Hungary. It is also inescapable that Wales – the subject of this book – shared strong linguistic connections with Gaul: Gaulish and Welsh are quite clearly very closely associated, as are Welsh and Breton. (For example, the number three in Welsh is *tri*, the same as Breton; four in Welsh is *pedwar*, in Breton *pevar*. The Gaulish celestial god 'Taranis' bears a 'thunder' name cognate with Welsh *taran*.) If we look at early medieval Wales, it can be seen that there are pre-Christian, pagan elements in the earliest mythic tales (in the *Pedeir Keinc y Mabinogi* and in *Culhwch ac Olwen*, for instance) that have shared motifs: the symbolic treatment of cauldrons is one apparently very clear link between the myths and the material culture of pagan Celtic Wales and much of temperate Europe; the symbolic importance of the human head is another. There is a sense, then, in which early Welsh traditions are embedded within a pre-Christian European context. In the chapters that follow, it is important to appreciate that, in antiquity, the region we know as Wales belonged within a broader setting and should, therefore, be studied against an essentially European backcloth.

2 The First Welsh Celts: Iron Age Wales

Tribes and settlement

The late Bronze Age background

In late Bronze Age Wales, there seems to have been a shift of population from upland regions toward coastal areas. This may have been, in large part, due to a combination of deteriorating climate and the destruction of the ecosystem through forest clearance on thin upland soils. These changes are suggested by archaeological evidence both in Wales and the west of England. By c. 1000 BC, for example, new social patterns are suggested by the emergence of a number of defended hilltop settlements in many areas. One region where these changes can be demonstrated is north Wales, particularly the northern marches, with important excavated sites like Breiddin in Powys and Moel y Gaer and Dinorben in Clwyd. At the latter, radiocarbon dates suggest that the first defensive rampart, made of alternating layers of timber-staging and clay or rubble, was built to enclose the site at the beginning of the first millennium BC.

These defended hilltop settlements are generally referred to as hillforts, and in the regions surrounding them it is often the case that a new type of bronze assemblage, including swords, spearheads and scabbards, has been found. Such artefacts may suggest Continental influences; they almost certainly imply increasing social instability. There is, for example, compelling evidence that objects such as leaf-shaped slashing swords and spears were being used. At Tormarton in Avon, near the border with Wales, the bodies of two young men who had been killed in about 1000 BC were found in what was, at the time of their death, a ditch. One had a hole through his pelvis apparently caused by a bronze spearhead. The second also had a hole through the pelvis as well as evidence of a severe head injury; a bronze spearhead was embedded in his spine!

There were interesting and probably important variations in late Bronze Age artefact assemblages. Hoards of distinctive spearheads have been found on several sites in the northern marches. In other parts of north Wales, an established centre for production of bronze implements, hoards of palstaves of late Bronze Age design

Map showing the position of the Celtic tribes in Wales at the time of the Roman conquest.

have been recovered. In south Wales, particularly Gwent and Glamorgan, distinctive socketed axes predominate in the archaeological record. It may be significant that these regional variations seem to approximate to later Iron Age tribal areas.

Early tribal groupings in Wales

By the time of the Roman invasion, Classical authorities refer to four main tribes in what is today Wales. The northern marches were home to a tribe called the Deceangli. Much of north Wales was held by the Ordovices, and southwest Wales by the Demetae. Gwent and Glamorgan were the homeland of the Silures who resisted the Roman advance with particular ferocity. It is likely that a number of sub-tribes also contributed to the mosaic of society in Iron Age Wales. Portions of modern Gwynedd, for example, may have been occupied by a people called the Gangani, possibly a sub-tribe of the Ordovices. The distribution of late Bronze Age metalwork seems to suggest that the origin of these tribes was early and that they pre-date the Iron Age, perhaps by a considerable period.

The advent of iron

The advent of iron production in Wales is difficult to date with confidence. A clue may lie in the ritual deposit at Llyn Fawr near Rhigos in Glamorgan which is considered in more depth in our discussion of ritual landscapes on p. 27. Among the items deposited were socketed axes and socketed sickles. The sickles may provide an important clue, since there are examples in both bronze and iron. The iron sickle seems to be a simple copy of the bronze design, a form less than wholly appropriate for an iron implement. If this is taken as evidence that the hoard represents very early iron production, we might reasonably conclude that the assumed deposition date of *c.* 700–600 BC is at or near the dawn of the Iron Age in Wales. However, it should be appreciated that, in addition to the iron objects, the Llyn Fawr hoard contained material usually assigned to the late Bronze Age, including socketed axes and sheet-bronze cauldrons. Accordingly, if the hoard was deposited as a single act, we either have to argue for a date for the first use of iron in Wales in the eighth–seventh century BC or to suggest that the late Bronze Age material was antique when the hoard was placed in the water. Alternatively, a better model for explaining the presence of the Llyn Fawr deposit is to propose episodic placement of metalwork over a long period of time.

Iron was soon used for a range of tools and weapons; there is a strong martial theme in many artefact assemblages. Swords, sometimes over 90cm in length, and spearheads are notable among items which have been found. So too are shield bosses such as those from Tal-y-llyn in Gwynedd and Moel Hiraddug in Clwyd. These bosses, replete with La Tène designs, were once mounted on large oblong wooden shields. Another important group of artefacts which is well represented in Iron Age Wales relates to horses. Horse trappings were important elements in the deposits at both Llyn Fawr and Llyn Cerrig Bach with harness fittings consisting of cheek-pieces for bridle bits and domed discs to decorate the harness of horse-drawn vehicles. At Llyn Cerrig Bach there were more than thirty fragments of iron chariot-wheel tyres, harness fittings, bridle bits and harness links. Horse trappings also featured in hoards from Abergele in Clwyd and Seven Sisters in Glamorgan as well as in isolated finds such as an inlaid enamel strap union found at Chepstow in Gwent.

Settlement sites

Finds such as the high-status metalwork described above inevit-ably shape our interpretation of Iron Age settlement sites, particularly the hillforts which dot the landscape of Wales. It is important to remember that there is a variety of settlement sites ranging from relatively small, presumably farmstead, settlements to the much larger, well-defended hilltop sites. Excavation on hillfort sites such as Moel y Gaer and Dinorben confirm multiple phases in construction and development, arguing for occupation over a long period. A second construction phase at Twyn y Gaer in northern Gwent may point to expansion by the Silures. Considerable attention in hillfort design was given to defence with elaborate systems of ramparts and multiple ditches eventually enclosing many of them. One of the earliest forms of hillfort defence was a simple palisade like the one which once surrounded Moel y Gaer. A variation employed at Dinorben was box ramparts consisting of soil from a ditch held between two rows of timber posts. The rows of vertical timbers were connected by horizontal ones making a box which provided a parapet for defenders. Both types of defence were employed as early as the eighth century BC. Later palisades were supported by sloping banks of earth added to the inside of the defences. Problems of rotting timbers and the dangers of fire were at least partially overcome by adopting these *glacis* defences; a deep ditch was dug and the removed soil dumped at the natural angle of slope to build up an inner rampart. Multiple ramparts eventually became common. Considerable attention was also given to entrances with easily defended curved entrance-passages or carefully contrived inturned gates, frequently with associated guard chambers, becoming common. Quantities of clay shot and suitable natural pebbles found at sites such as Maiden Castle indicate that slings were one of the weapons used to guard these entrances.

Excavation reveals that the interior of hillforts is often dominated by postholes for timbers defining roundhouses which typify the British Iron Age. The pattern in the location of these roundhouses often suggests that there was deliberate planning in their arrangement. In addition, there are frequently a number of four-post structures which are generally interpreted as raised granaries. These corn stores suggest successful farming communities producing grain surpluses, a view supported by field patterns identified in areas like north Wales. As well as evidence for arable production, there are also clear indications that pastoral activities were important in most parts of Wales. Small circular enclosures found near hillforts in north Wales, for example, probably served as stock-pens. The same is probably also true of annexes to hillforts such as those at Llanmelin in Gwent. Among other features recovered by excavation of hillfort sites are large clay-lined pits which may have acted as reservoirs. A square pond at Breiddin, for example, could have secured the water supply of that hillfort.

Not all of the major enclosed Iron Age sites in Wales were hillforts. Promontory forts along the coastline were also important; a case in point is Coygan Camp, an excavated site between Laugharne and Pendine in Dyfed. Another important, but only partially excavated, site is Sudbrook Camp, located between the Severn Bridges in Gwent. Here a large rampart and three parallel ditches enclosed a site ideally suited to become a focus for trade in the Bristol Channel.

Smaller settlement sites can provide particular insights into rural society. In south-west Wales, for example, relatively small, generally round earthworks called raths are widespread. Excavation of one of these, Walesland Rath near Haverfordwest in Dyfed, confirmed that the enclosed area of 64m by 49m once

Goldcliff

Another particularly interesting Iron Age site is Goldcliff on the Gwent Levels which was investigated by field survey and excavation, 1990–5. Excavation on the site was especially difficult as it is located within the intertidal area; the site is covered by the sea twice a day and has a difficult mud cover of varying thickness. Among the features identified were a number of rectangular structures, brushwood trackways and linear features defined by small vertical posts. The largest of the rectangular structures was 6m by 8m, defined by uprights of roundwood and split timber. The structure had rounded corners and pairs of post groupings down its long axis, strongly suggesting roof supports. The site may indicate seasonal occupation and confirms land utilization of the levels in the Iron Age. The rectangularity of the structures preserved at Goldcliff is noteworthy, given the almost universal pattern of roundhouse building in Iron Age Britain. Rectangular forms are, by contrast, the norm for the Continental Iron Age.

contained at least three timber structures as well as a range of smaller buildings, some freestanding and some built against the rampart. Similar arrangements may have existed at Llwyn Du Bach and Castell Odo in Gwynedd. Particularly interesting are a series of eleven well-defined earthworks near Llawhaden in Dyfed. The enclosures all seem to have belonged to small farmsteads located within a two-square-mile area. Such close proximity raises questions about the nature of the social structure, and it is at least an interesting possibility that these sites might suggest that *cyfran,* inheritance by gavelkind where all sons benefited equally, was already being practised in the Iron Age. This system of partible inheritance became a key feature of Welsh medieval law.

Work like that by Martin Bell at Goldcliff on the Gwent Levels has improved our understanding of Iron Age Wales, but there are still many questions about the nature of Iron Age settlement in Wales and about the function of sites such as hillforts which cannot be answered at present. The nature of hillfort occupation is by no means clear. It is attractive to see these sites as large defended settlements with relatively stable populations. Estimates based on foundations of roundhouses in north Wales on sites such as Tre'r

Bryn Eryr

An enclosed rural settlement has been the subject of excavations at Bryn Eryr on Anglesey, where in the fifth century BC a single clay-walled roundhouse was erected within a timber palisade. About a hundred or so years later a second circular house was added next to the first. The two houses were the focus of an organized 'smallholding' contained within a rectangular banked and ditched enclosure. A trackway connected the house-fronts to a yard. Associated post-built rectangular granaries and clay-pits were identified by the excavators. In the early first millennium AD, the bank and ditch ceased to be maintained; a new, stone-footed roundhouse was constructed to the south of the original two and one of the latter was abandoned. Despite the apparent continued simplicity of lifestyle, the inhabitants of the Romano-British house were sufficiently prosperous to be able to afford a small amount of good-quality commodities, including samian pottery and glass. The economy of the farmstead was mixed: quernstones are indicative of grain-processing; the normal range of domestic animals was present, with the interesting exception of pigs.

Ceiri, Garn Boduan and Conwy Mountain, for example, have suggested that communities of between 100 and 400 people could have lived within the enclosure. Caution, however, is required. It seems reasonable to assume that an agricultural community would have wished to farm in productive lowland areas. One model would be that such lowland farmers would have seen the hillforts as temporary refuges and defended storage areas and that occupation of the hillfort would have been transient. Another interpretation could be that the hillfort represented an élite site with a warrior-aristocracy dominating the surrounding countryside and controlling surpluses. The hillforts could have been trading centres with a range of 'central space' functions. Similarly, they could have served as craft production centres, marketplaces, foci for religious rituals, or other activities. In reality, hillforts could have served any or all of these functions and could have had different functions at different times. More evidence, derived from careful excavation of selected sites, is needed to allow us to refine our interpretations. This need is particularly acute in the south-east where very little work has been done in the second half of the twentieth century. Yet, despite the limited evidence, we can point with some confidence to the existence of a tribal people who practised sophisticated farming techniques which regularly produced surpluses (these sometimes leading to the adoption of the trappings of Roman civilization following the Roman occupation (see chapter 3)) and to a range of enclosed settlement sites including large and well-defended hillforts.

Trade and Commerce

A maritime tradition

Evidence for Bronze Age origins of Iron Age tribal structures argues for a high degree of cultural continuity. However, Iron Age communities in Wales did not develop in a vacuum and there is compelling evidence for trade contacts not only with other parts of Britain but also with the Continent, including the Classical world. There is certainly good evidence for travel by water in the Bronze Age; a notable example is the Caergwrle bowl which is thought to date from around 1200 BC. A particularly impressive example of prehistoric craftsmanship, the bowl represents a boat with gunwales, oars and a keel. Made of incised shale filled with tin, the bowl was covered in gold foil. The impressive detail on the bowl extends to 'waves' running along the hull of the boat!

The 'golden' boat from Caergwrle is significant in confirming craft and artistry as well as providing a potent symbol of trade. This north Wales find complements the excavation of boat fragments from the Gwent Levels in south Wales. A fragment of a Bronze Age boat has been excavated at Caldicot as have two planks at Goldcliff. All seem to have been from sewn boats with hull constructions not unlike the *mtepe* dhows still found in the Indian Ocean today. Such boats could have been usefully employed in trading voyages across the Bristol Channel.

Trade and cultural interaction

As has been seen, promontory forts such as Sudbrook were well placed to act as ports for such seaborne trade. At Coygan Camp, a pair of bronze La Tène bracelets on a copper core were found in the excavations conducted between 1963 and 1965. The bracelets are similar to examples from the Continent and, perhaps even more interestingly, also to two smaller ones which were excavated in the inner defensive ditch at Llanmelin, a hillfort on high ground to the north of Sudbrook Camp. It is tempting to see both sets of bracelets as trade goods, unless they were the product of gift-exchange mechanisms.

The Cerrigydrudion bowl, originally interpreted as a hanging bowl but now thought by some experts to be a lid or helmet, is generally viewed as an import. If so, it was a part of a well-documented system binding the south-west of England, and almost certainly Wales, with Brittany and the Atlantic coastal regions of France in a complex trading network. Central to this network were the maritime Veneti, the tribe from southern Brittany who traded not only with Britain through such ports as Hengistbury Head in Dorset but also with southern France and the Mediterranean. There was also an important trade route between the south-east of England and the Continent. Strabo described the short trading journey between Britain and Gaul at the end of the first century BC, writing 'people who set sail on the ebb tide in the evening, land on the island at about the eighth hour on the following day'. According to Strabo, goods coming from Britain in the very late Iron Age included grain, cattle, gold, silver, iron, hides, slaves and hunting dogs. Luxury items such as ivory necklaces, amber and glass vessels were popular in return. Wine was a particularly important import. As the Roman writer Diodorus Siculus observed, 'they are exceedingly fond of wine and sate themselves with the unmixed wine imported by merchants'. In parts of Britain, discoveries of amphorae, large Roman wine containers, confirm a regular long-distance wine trade between Britain and the Continent. An interesting artefact which may be a legacy of a trading voyage is a lead anchor stock which was found off the coast of the Llŷn peninsula. The stock, which was found off Porth Felen, is thought to have been of Mediterranean origin; it may have been lost from a trading vessel which set sail in the late second or early first century BC. Given widespread evidence for trade, it seems likely that Wales was part of an Atlantic trading community and it may be that at times the Veneti played a particularly important role in linking western Britain with Iron Age communities on the Continent as well as with the Classical world.

Religion and ritual

Ritual landscapes

The best evidence for ritual practice in Iron Age Wales consists of deposition in watery contexts. Llyn Fawr and Llyn Cerrig Bach are two aquatic sites whose deposits of metalwork and organic remains are highly suggestive of ritual action. Interestingly, these sites are situated at opposite ends of Wales: Llyn Fawr near Rhigos in Glamorgan and Llyn Cerrig Bach near Llanfair-yn-neubwll on the island of Anglesey. The two sites also represent opposite ends of the Iron Age chronological spectrum: the metalwork assemblage found at Llyn Fawr dates to the eighth–seventh century BC, that at Llyn Cerrig to between the second century BC and the first century AD.

The site of Llyn Cerrig Bach on Anglesey consisted of a deposit of metalwork and other objects found by chance during construction work. The discoveries were made in 1943 when the

Discoveries at Llyn Fawr

The Llyn Fawr metalwork was discovered in 1911 during its conversion to a reservoir. The assemblage included a pair of cauldrons made of riveted, beaten sheet-bronze plates, socketed axes (their decoration suggestive of an origin in south-east England rather than of local manufacture), two socketed bronze sickles, a socketed, wrought-iron sickle, a wrought-iron socketed spearhead and a fragmentary Hallstatt C iron sword. Apparently all the pieces were found grouped together, embedded in the peat, with the exception of one of the cauldrons. The implications are, firstly, that the assemblage represents collective, though perhaps episodic, acts of deposition and, secondly, that part of the hoard was originally contained in the cauldron found with it. The metalwork belongs to the horizon of the late Bronze Age/early Iron Age transition: some pieces, like the cauldrons, were of local manufacture and others, like the iron sword, were exotic to the region. As well as the bronze and iron objects, it was reported at the time of discovery that a number of hazelnuts and pieces of birch bark were also recovered, well preserved and embedded in the peat.

ground was being prepared for the RAF Valley airfield, which required peat from the nearby peat-bog, and it is likely that there is still more material in the marsh. The deposit recovered comprises a large body of metalwork, of some 144 pieces. Unlike the Llyn Fawr assemblage, the diverse chronology of the material suggests that it accumulated at Llyn Cerrig as the result of episodic deposition in the lake over a period of some two hundred years, from *c.* 150 BC to AD 50. The Llyn Cerrig assemblage consists of predominantly high-status martial equipment, some of it finely decorated bronzework, including a crescentric sheet-bronze plaque ornamented in repoussé with a bird-head triskele and a finely engraved bronze shield-boss, swords and scabbards (one with a maker's name stamped on the blade and some stamped with motifs or symbols), spearheads, a dagger, chariot-fittings, including several iron tyres, horse-gear, a bronze trumpet, spiral bindings from two bronze sceptres, iron-smithing and agricultural tools, iron currency bars and two wrought-iron slave gang-chains.

In addition to the metalwork, a quantity of animal-bone was recovered, of which only a small proportion was collected and retained at the time. The bones include those of a small, pony-sized equine (appropriate for pulling a light chariot of the type represented by the Llyn Cerrig fittings), cattle, sheep and dog. Three bones were sampled in the early 1990s for radiocarbon dating by the Oxford University Accelerator Unit, and have yielded some interesting results, with dates ranging between 500 and 400 BC (calibrated). This means that, if accurate and if the metalwork has been correctly dated on stylistic grounds, the animal-bones arrived in the lake as the result of events separated by at least 200 years from the deposition of the metal objects. It is tempting to interpret this chronological disparity as the result of changing depositional practices wherein the sacrifice of animals was – largely or wholly – replaced by the votive offering of prestige bronze and iron equipment to the supernatural powers.

Despite the differences between Llyn Fawr and Llyn Cerrig, in terms of assemblage and chronology, the essential similarities are very clear: both were watery sites in antiquity; each site would have been relatively remote; the metalwork in both included valuable, high-status material that would not have been discarded as rubbish; each deposit contained substantive amounts of metal-work; each contained a mixture of bronze and iron objects; and both assemblages included pairs of cauldrons.

It is generally accepted that both assemblages are best understood as ritual deposits in watery contexts from which the material, once cast in, was never intended to be recovered. The assemblages cannot have been treasuries, similar to the great Classical temple-treasuries such as existed under the guardianship of Apollo at Delphi, precisely because the metalwork would have sunk irrecoverably into the water and mud under its own weight. The deposits at Llyn Fawr and Llyn Cerrig need to be interpreted within a much wider context of ritual water-deposition of high-value, frequently military, equipment that took place over a wide area within temperate and northern Europe and occurred spasm-odically over a long time span, during the later Bronze Age and episodically during the Iron Age. Llyn Fawr and Llyn Cerrig Bach have their parallels outside Wales, for instance at Loughnashade in northern Ireland, a lake into which, in the later Iron Age, four superbly crafted bronze ceremonial trumpets had been cast as a ritual act, and at Flag Fen in Cambridgeshire where, during the later Bronze Age, a kilometre-long line of timber posts was constructed in the waters of the fen edge, associated with some 300 bronze – mainly military – artefacts, most of which had suffered deliberate and ritual damage (like some of the gear from Llyn Cerrig), together with ceramic and faunal remains. Nearby was an artificial island consisting of a timber platform on which the local community probably built their houses. The posts and platform at Flag Fen were in use for about four hundred years, but the custom of ritual deposition took place over a much longer time zone that spanned at least a thousand years. Llyn Cerrig Bach, perhaps, was likewise the focus of long-lasting, episodic ritual activity, though for a shorter period, but Llyn Fawr – by contrast – may represent a single act of deposition, or repeated ritual over a relatively short period.

Besides multiple deposition of valuable material in watery locations, a number of spectacular finds of single Iron Age objects in pools or marshes have been made in Wales; these are arguably part of the same ritual tradition that gave rise to the assemblages at Llyn Fawr and Llyn Cerrig. They include items of prestige equipment associated, like the cauldrons at the two major sites, with aristocratic feasting and must have represented valuable gifts to the spirit world. One such object is the great decorative wrought-iron fire-dog with bull's-head terminals from Capel Garmon in north Wales, a piece of high-status hearth-furniture of first century AD date; this had been deposited in a pool, a large stone carefully placed at each end. The fire-dog is a superb piece of

Yew-wood, bronze-covered tankard, found in a peat-bog at Trawsfynydd in north Wales; first century AD. It was probably used to hold liquor at communal feasts. Ht. 14.3cm.

craftsmanship that may represent as much as three years' work for a single smith. Although several bull-headed iron fire-dogs are recorded from British Iron Age sites, the Capel Garmon example is unique in the elaborate manes worn by the two slender-horned bulls, giving them an ambiguous, horse-like appearance. It is interesting to note that the supernatural bulls described in the great pagan Irish epic known as the *Táin Bó Cuailnge*, compiled in written form during the later first millennium AD, are referred to as possessing long, decorative manes.

Of similar date and context to the Capel Garmon deposit is the find from Trawsfynydd, once again in a north Wales watery location. This is yet another high-status, arguably ceremonial, item of feasting-equipment, a large yew-wood tankard covered in sheet-bronze, with a highly ornamental handle. The size of this vessel – the rim measures 184mm maximum – argues for its use as a communal drinking-cup, perhaps passed round during feasting ceremonies, which may have acted as socio-religious bonding activities. Like the bronze-covered stave-built buckets – of roughly coeval date – from high-ranking cremation-graves in south-east England (for instance at Marlborough and Aylesford) such tankards may have been designed to hold beer, mead or berry juice rather than wine.

The repeated deposition of prestigious goods in watery contexts undoubtedly reflects highly ritualized action associated, perhaps, with the episodic renewal of allegiance to the spirit-powers perceived as residing in remote, liminal, dangerous and inaccessible places such as pools and bogs. This practice may have acted, at one and the same time, as a bonding mechanism for local groups, a means of renewing ties with the gods and – in times of particular need – a symbolic way of propitiating the supernatural powers.

Water-ritual at the Breiddin

The main rampart of the hillfort known as the Breiddin, in the Welsh Marches, was probably built in the third century BC. To the same period belongs a large rectangular cistern which was constructed at one end of a natural pond in the centre of the enclosed area. Investigation by the Clwyd–Powys Archaeological Trust revealed a number of wooden objects which may have been cast into the cistern as a votive act. Material found in the water included wooden vessels and a curious wooden 'sword'. This last piece could have been specially made as a functionless and, therefore, sacred object, in much the same way as other offerings to the supernatural powers could take the form of deliberately broken or miniature implements and weapons, which were equally devoid of practical use.

Images of the gods

Very little, if any, religious iconography can be assigned, with any confidence, to Iron Age Wales; the few images we have cannot be precisely dated. Thus, the carved stone heads from Hendy (Llanfair Pwllgwyngyll), Llanallgo and Llangeinwen on Anglesey and from Carmarthen in Dyfed by no means certainly belong to the pre-Roman Iron Age and, indeed, the Anglesey heads might even be medieval. If the heads are of Iron Age or Roman date, they belong within a very widespread tradition of human-head representation that can be traced over a large area, from Ireland to Central Europe; many of the stone heads come from northern Britain. The heads are likely to have represented local divinities, and the practice of depicting the head alone may relate to the testimony of Classical writers on the Gauls, for whom the human head had special significance. These Graeco-Roman authors also speak of the ritual collection of enemy heads as trophies; this may account for the numerous fragments of human skulls recovered from excavations at the Dinorben hillfort in north Wales, a phenomenon recorded also at other British Iron Age hillforts.

Shrines and burial places

No structures that are clearly identifiable as Iron Age sanctuaries are known in Wales. However, it is possible that the Romano-British shrine discovered by aerial reconnaissance at Gwehelog in south-east Wales had pre-Roman ancestry. The hoard of Roman bronzes found by metal detector at Llys Awel, Abergele in 1979/80, which includes several votive objects, must have come originally from a Romano-British cult-establishment that may – likewise – have stood on the site of an earlier sanctuary; the same may also be true of the probable Romano-Celtic temple found, again, by aerial photography near Ruthin in the Vale of Clwyd.

In line with several areas of Iron Age Britain, it is likely that pre-Roman shrines in Wales defy clear identification as such, partly because of the absence of a formalized religious architecture, partly on account of the sparse evidence for distinctive ritual action on dry sites. In this connection, it is worth mentioning the site of Thornwell Farm, near Chepstow, which contained a pre-Roman Iron Age roundhouse of substantial build, some 12.5m in diameter. The excavators noted not only that the two halves of the encircling wall were constructed differently one from the other, but that the patterning of finds in the two halves seemed also to mark divergent functions between them. Such asymmetry suggested to the investigating team that respective demarcation of secular and sacred space might be present. Such a model, based ultimately on ethnographic comparanda, is currently being applied to other 'domestic' circular structures elsewhere in Iron Age Britain.

Few Iron Age cemeteries are recorded in Wales. Complete or partial inhumation burials of later Iron Age date are known to have been associated with settlements, for instance at Dinorben and Moel Hiraddug in the north, Coygan and Stackpole in the south-west and Llanmelin in the south-east. A few very late Iron Age high-status graves, comparable to the 'Welwyn' or 'Aylesford-Swarling' tombs of south-east England, can be identified: a slab-built warrior-grave, with a skeleton and iron sword, has been found at Gelliniog Wen on Anglesey, the only such burial at present recorded in Wales. The finely decorated bronze known as the 'Cerrigydrudion Bowl' (probably, in fact, part of a lid), also from north Wales, allegedly accompanied an inhumation grave, and two other late burials accompanied by mirrors come from Llechwedd Du Bach in Gwynedd and Llanwnda in Dyfed. Finally, reference should be made to the few instances of human remains associated with Iron Age material in caves: one of these is Culverhole, on the Gower coast; this cave also produced a Romano-British bronze figurine of a nursing mother-goddess.

Human sacrifice and the Druids

> The enemy lined the shore in a dense armed mass. Among them were black-robed women with dishevelled hair like Furies, brandishing torches. Close by stood Druids, raising their hands to heaven and screaming dreadful curses . . . Suetonius garrisoned the conquered island. The groves devoted to Mona's barbarous superstitions he demolished. For it was their religion to drench their altars in the blood of prisoners and consult their gods by means of human entrails. (Tacitus, *Annales* XIV, 30–1)

So wrote the imperial Roman chronicler Cornelius Tacitus in the early second century AD, recording events that took place on Anglesey, in the extreme western corner of the Roman Empire in the mid-first century AD. Tacitus is generally regarded as a relatively reliable source, and he is unlikely to have invented either the confrontation or the presence of the Druids. We learn from Julius Caesar, writing a hundred years earlier, that the Druids existed in Britain as well as in Gaul and he comments that their origins lay there. The passage in the Annals is significant inasmuch as it specifically links the Druids with the human sacrifice of prisoners, a cult-practice also recorded for Gaul (*De Bello Gallico* VI, 16) and North Germany (Strabo, *Geographia* VII, 2, 3). Clearly, it is

Early twentieth-century picture of the Druids confronting the Roman army, as they defend their sacred island of Anglesey in AD *61. The scene is based on Tacitus' narrative, and first appeared in Dudley Wright's* Druidism, The Ancient Faith of Britain *(London, 1924).*

impossible to find archaeological evidence that corroborates such statements – either on the presence of the Druids in Wales (or anywhere else) or the ritual murder of human victims – but it is permissible to point to circumstantial data to support both. The ritual deposition of the high-status equipment and animal sacrifices discussed earlier are suggestive of an organized religious structure within Iron Age Wales, and formalized cult-systems are usually dependent upon a professional clergy or priestly class with strong sacro-political influence in their societies. Caesar says as much (VI, 13–14) when he describes the multifarious functions of the Druids in Gaul.

Our best candidates for human sacrifice in western Britain belong to the very late Iron Age and earlier Roman period. These are two ancient male bog-bodies from Lindow Moss in Cheshire, a few miles east of the present Welsh border, discovered between 1983 and 1988 (known as Lindow II and Lindow III). Although there have been serious problems over the radiocarbon analysis of the Lindow Moss material, the latest results suggest that Lindow II (otherwise known as 'Pete Marsh') was killed during the first century AD and Lindow III about a hundred years later. Lindow II was a well-nourished man of about twenty-five; he had been placed face down in a shallow bog-pool, naked except for a fox-fur armlet, after suffering two severe blows to the head which cracked his skull, strangulation and throat-slitting. The preservation of his stomach and gut revealed that, just before his death, he partook of a 'special' meal: a coarse, griddle-baked loaf containing many different seeds and cereal grains, including mistletoe pollen; he had also drunk water from the marsh. Was this individual executed for some criminal, anti-social or sacriligious act, or was he a human sacrifice killed, perhaps, in order to avert an impending disaster to his community? His neatly trimmed moustache, manicured fingernails and painted skin, all preserved by the anaerobic conditions of the marsh, suggest that he was a person of some rank. What catastrophe could have triggered such a ritual murder, if such it be, is impossible to say, but Lindow Moss is situated close to the route taken by Suetonius Paulinus' army marching from the south-east to crush the Druidic stronghold on Anglesey in AD 61, as told by Tacitus. Could the local community have sacrificed one of its high-ranking members in a desperate attempt to halt Paulinus' forces by a supreme gift?

Lindow III provides equally enigmatic and fascinating information, although it is even less easy to link the killing with a historical event. The body of this later victim, taller and a little older than Lindow II, had also been painted; his head had been severed, although whether this decapitation was the cause of death or occurred postmortem is unknown. His fingernails also attested to his non-peasant status and, what is more, he was special in his possession of a vestigial second thumb. Like Lindow II, his gut bore testimony to his consumption of a singular meal, this time consisting largely of crushed hazelnuts. We need to be careful before jumping to conclusions concerning the ritual nature of this meal, since hazelnuts, when available, must have been eaten as a regular part of the diet, but we should also remember that hazel appears to have had a symbolism associated with water and, specifically, with bog-bodies. For example, an Iron Age bog-victim from Ireland had been strangled with a garotte made of hazel withies, and hazel rods were associated with some Scandinavian marsh-bodies; the Llyn Fawr deposit included hazel, again linking the plant with aquatic ritual. This link between hazel and water symbolism is especially interesting in the light of an inscribed lead curse-tablet, of late Roman date, from Brandon in East Anglia, which appeals for justice from 'Neptune with hazel'. Evidence for the symbolic significance of hazel in a later, 'historical', context comes from the early medieval group of mythic tales known as the Fenian Cycle which, although its earliest recension dates to the twelfth century AD, its overt paganism argues for a far earlier genesis. One episode describes the means by which the Salmon of Knowledge gained its wisdom: by eating the fruit of nine hazel trees growing beside a well at the bottom of the sea.

Although it is possible to argue against a sacrificial end for the two Lindow bog-bodies, it is difficult to explain away in terms of purely secular deaths the combination of their nakedness, the complex nature of their injuries and their watery deposition. We have the repeated testimony of Graeco-Roman writers for human sacrifice among the Gauls, Germans and Britons in the late first millennium BC and Tacitus even refers to ritual dispatch, by immersion in marshes, of individuals found guilty of deviant behaviour. Whilst it is unwise to cite these two bog-victims as unequivocal evidence for human sacrifice, the balance of probability must surely lie in favour of such an interpretation.

Celtic art in Iron Age Wales

The Iron Age site of La Tène, on the shore of Lake Neuchâtel in Switzerland, has given its name to a widespread tradition of geometric art that was mainly produced between the fifth century BC and the first century AD, in much of temperate and northern Europe. This art-tradition, which used plant, animal and – to a much lesser extent – human form as a base from which to develop a highly individual set of 'abstract' designs, generally survives on high-status metalwork, but is known also to have decorated humbler objects, such as quernstones and domestic pottery. Interestingly, although this art-style largely disappeared in mainland Europe under the very different – life-copying – traditions of imperial Rome, this is not true for the western periphery of the Celtic world. Ireland was never made part of the Roman Empire, and large areas of Wales and Scotland were never fully integrated into the romanized world; in these regions, Celtic art continued to flourish during the earlier first millennium AD and, in Ireland, Celtic artistic traditions can be found in the rich monastic Christian art of the illuminated manuscripts, church plate and decorated stone crosses of the medieval period.

In Wales, as in Scotland, La Tène art flourished late, compared to that of Continental Europe. Most of the art from Wales was produced late in the La Tène sequence, during the first centuries BC and AD. The preserved artwork decorates objects that are almost all prestigious equipment – like the first-century-AD collar-fragment, with cast scroll patterns, from near Llandysul in Dyfed – and many of them (see p. 27) were probably deposited in a manner suggesting their dedication as votive gifts to the divine powers. One of the earliest pieces is the fragmentary bronzework from a burial cist at Cerrigydrudion in Clwyd, of fourth century BC date. The pieces were long considered part of a bowl, but more recently have been reinterpreted as belonging either to a lid or a helmet. The flange of the so-called 'bowl' is ornamented with curvilinear, plant-derived motifs; metallurgical analysis suggests that the object was produced in Brittany.

More enigmatic than any of the aforementioned objects are the two pairs of bronze spoons with decorative handles from Castell Nadolig in Dyfed, whose embossed ornament compares closely with the technique displayed on the Llyn Cerrig plaque, and from Ffynnogion in Clwyd. Pairs of spoons like these have been found in graves elsewhere in Britain, and certain distinct and curious features of these items suggest their ritual purpose, notably the small holes placed in different positions on each spoon, and the way one of the pair is divided into quadrants by means of incised lines.

The symbolic triskele (Welsh trisgell)

One of the most recurrent designs on Welsh art is the triskele, a triple-armed, whirling motif whose ubiquity, not only in Wales but also throughout Europe, suggests its symbolic significance (particularly in view of the prominence of triplism in later Romano-Celtic cult iconography). The crescentric plaque from Llyn Cerrig Bach has an asymmetrical triskele with very stylized bird-head terminals, and an engraved bronze shield-boss from the site is adorned with a meandering version of the three-armed motif: both probably date to the first century BC. Yet another triskele adorns a shield-boss and several openwork discs from the hoard of scrap-metal from Tal-y-llyn in Gwynedd, produced in the first century AD; of the same date is a rectilinear plaque from Moel Hiraddug in Clwyd, ornamented with a curious, angled or 'broken-backed' triskele, and the Trawsfynydd tankard, whose handle bears a triskele motif.

The Welsh Iron Age art described so far is largely composed of abstract patterns, although ultimately derived from plant-designs. However, some art is more overtly based on animal-forms. The enamelled handle of a bowl from Snowdon, dated to the first century AD, takes the form of a superbly crafted cat's face, paralleled in Britain only by a cat's-head mirror-handle from Holcombe in Devon. A series of bucket-escutcheons, in the form of cattle-heads come from the hillfort at Dinorben, near Abergele in Clwyd, Welshpool in Powys, and a cache of five from the Little Orme in Gwynedd. Such decoration, on large vessels that were perhaps used in feasting, brings to mind another bull-decorated piece of banqueting equipment, the iron fire-dog from Capel Garmon (see p. 29).

Human imagery appears seldom on Welsh Iron Age art, and this reflects the paucity of anthropomorphic forms present in La Tène art as a whole. The exception, as is true for Britain and Europe, is the human head. Stone heads are known from Anglesey

One of two trapezoidal bronze plaques depicting conjoined human faces framed by leaf-patterns, possibly once adorning shields. From a hoard of metalwork found at Tal-y-llyn, north Wales; first century ad.

and Carmarthen; a water-rolled pebble from the River Twymyn at Bontdolgadfan, Llanbrynmair in Powys bears roughly incised human features. These depictions which probably, though not certainly, pre-date the Roman period are matched in metal by the twin plaques from the assemblage of metalwork buried as a scrap hoard at Tal-y-llyn in the first century AD; the presence of brass – thought to be a Roman innovation – may point to a post-conquest date. Each plaque bears a double head joined by a single, long neck, each head enclosed by a leaf-pattern. Human depictions are sufficiently rare for their valid, if tentative, interpretation as the images of divinities. The schematized features of all the Welsh heads assigned to the Iron Age in Wales anticipate stone examples of Roman date, such as that of the seated goddess and the severed head from Caerwent.

3 Celts and Romans

Conquest and conflict: the Roman invasions

Iron Age societies in Britain interacted with those on the Continent and, as has been seen, tribes in Wales were, at least to an extent, part of an Atlantic trading community with links to the Classical world. By the 50s BC, however, the nature of that relationship was changing rapidly in response to the aggressive expansion of Rome. In 56 BC, Julius Caesar attempted to consolidate his victories in Gaul and struck against the Veneti, the maritime Breton tribe which dominated the western trade route. The destruction of the Venetic fleet had a profound impact on

The first invasions

Caesar's invasion of 55 BC was strongly resisted. The invasion fleet eventually attempted to land, probably near Deal (Kent), in the face of hostile defenders supported by cavalry and chariots. Despite establishing a bridgehead, the Romans were unable to land their cavalry because of storms and, with winter approaching, could not consolidate any advantage. Caesar withdrew to Gaul and the Roman senate proclaimed a period of thanksgiving for what could, at best, be described as a moderate military success. Caesar had, however, learned from the experience. Damaged vessels were repaired and new ships were built including 600 transports and twenty-eight new shallow-draft warships designed to land troops quickly. Also available for the invasion of 54 BC were five legions supported by some 2,000 cavalry. This massive force landed unopposed and, despite determined opposition, defeated the Catuvellauni and crossed the Thames. Having established a measure of military control in the south-east of England, Caesar demanded tribute and hostages and then returned to Gaul where fears of revolt were growing. Soon war with Vercingetorix removed any likelihood that the Romans would return to Britain in the near future.

patterns of trade; it may also have been a factor in persuading Caesar to invade Britain in the following year.

The immediate impact of Caesar's invasions on the peoples of Wales was negligible. It was not long, however, before significant changes began to permeate the whole of Britain. Some south-eastern tribes aligned themselves to Rome as clients and this may have been a factor in stimulating trade. The nature of the trade, however, changed. New political orientations and the destruction of the Venetic fleet saw the once important western trade route, which had fostered the Atlantic trading community, decline while cross-channel trade to the south-east increased. Another interesting, and probably related, change was a growth in coin use. A number of tribes began to mint coins and, while there is no evidence that Welsh tribes ever did so, some coins from other areas have been found in Wales. This is particularly true in the south-east where coins of the Dobunni have been found at places like Caldicot, Chepstow, Dingestow, Llanthony and Whitton. The Dobunnic coins frequently had striking iconography; for example, a find from Tintern has a stylized horse on one side and the head of a stalk of grain on the other. It is interesting to note that many of the finds from Welsh sites are gold coins and the distribution pattern, in so far as one can be established, differs from that in Dobunnic regions where many more lower denomination silver coins predominate. Assuming that the gold coins would have far too high a value for most normal transactions, the Silures seem to have had limited and specific use for the coins which were probably seen as a useful way to store and/or transmit wealth.

In south-eastern Britain, the century between the invasions by Caesar and the return of the legions saw a range of complicated political manoeuvres. Among the most important factors was continuing tension between the Catuvellauni and the Trinovantes. Eventually the Catuvellauni led by Cunobelinus triumphed and, perhaps in part because of its importance in controlling trade routes, took Camulodunum (Colchester). Although never clients of Rome, the Catuvellauni seem to have maintained the flourishing trade contacts with the Continent which were sustained through the life of Cunobelinus. However, his death, sometime between AD 40 and 43, precipitated events which contributed to a new Roman military intervention. The sons of Cunobelinus, Togodumnus and Caratacus (Caradog), succeeded their father, with the former becoming king in lands north of the Thames. The brothers were anti-Roman and this, combined with the growing political domination of the Catuvellauni, was probably a factor in encouraging the Romans to intervene in Britain. There were other 'domestic' reasons. The unlikely emperor Claudius had been placed on the throne by a military coup in AD 41. Given the extravagance of his predecessor, Gaius, the new emperor needed money, particularly to assure the continuing loyalty of the army. Booty from the conquest of Britain could provide a much-needed boost to the imperial exchequer. Even more important was the emperor's need to secure his position by victory in war. It was no surprise that the professional soldiers who achieved victory in the invasion of southern England stood aside for Claudius himself to take command for the final entry into Camulodunum after the initial military issues had been decided.

The invasion of Britain in AD 43 was undertaken by a massive military force commanded by Aulus Plautius who came from a governorship on the Danube. With him were leading legionary commanders who included the future emperor Vespasian. The core of the invading army was four legions, three of which were moved from the Rhine frontier for the British campaign. These included II Augusta which had been stationed in Strasbourg, XIV Gemina which had been at Mainz and XX Valeria Victrix which was moved from Cologne. The fourth legion, which accompanied Plautius when he took up his new command, was IX Hispana from Pannonia. The invading army also consisted of large numbers of auxiliaries, non-Roman troops raised throughout the empire. These auxiliaries provided trained archers as well as cavalry and were an important element in an invasion force which consisted of over 40,000 men. Some of these auxiliaries are identified by the Roman historian Cassius Dio as 'Celtic' and they were to play a key role in several decisive encounters.

The invading army landed unopposed and initially faced only skirmishes with small forces led by Caratacus and Togodumnus. These skirmishes were probably intended to delay the advancing Romans so that a large native force could be massed on the River Medway. There a two-day battle raged which was only won by the Romans when Celtic auxiliaries managed to cross the river and shoot down the chariot horses of the defenders. In the ensuing confusion, Vespasian crossed with heavily armed legionary forces who scattered the Britons. Nevertheless, they continued to skirmish as they retreated towards the Thames. There were heavy casualties on both sides and it was in one of these running battles that Togodumnus was killed. Notwithstanding the loss of their leader, the tribesmen continued to resist despite the arrival of Claudius with an entourage including elephants for a show of splendour as he staged his triumphal entry into Camulodunum. Before long, however, the concentration of organized and disciplined Roman military power led to the collapse of the resistance of the south-eastern tribes; the main centres of power of the Catuvellauni were taken and tribes like the Dobunni sued for peace. Some tribes, notably in the west, did continue to resist. Among those that did so were the Durotriges of Dorset and the archaeological evidence suggests that there was heavy fighting at hillforts like Maiden Castle. Nevertheless, within five years or so, effective Roman control had been established over southern England. Wales, however, was a different matter. Dismayed by the collapse of the resistance in the south-east, Caratacus fled west to rally anti-Roman forces. He was naturally drawn to the warlike Silures of south Wales and soon this area became the centre of resistance to the Roman advance. In response, the military might of Rome was turned toward Wales.

The Silurian war

The successful invading general Aulus Plautius was appointed as the first governor of Britain and he spent some four years consolidating the Roman position and creating a new province in the fertile 'lowland zone' of Britain. Stunned by the size and ferocity of the Roman invasion, the south-eastern tribes seemed reconciled to the new order. This was not a view shared by the more hostile tribes beyond the conquered regions and in AD 47, in an attempt to capitalize on the appointment of a new governor, Publius Ostorius Scapula, they attacked. Despite the fact that winter had begun, Ostorius responded immediately. He set out to reduce the whole of the territory between the Severn and the Trent but was thwarted by a revolt of the Iceni of East Anglia. Relying heavily on auxiliary troops, Ostorius put down the Icenian revolt, but in doing so he sowed seeds of hatred which would contribute to an even greater rebellion more than a decade later. In the short term, however, his success allowed him to strike against the western tribes and he attacked the Deceangli of north-east Wales. He drove deeply into the territory of the Welsh tribe and, in the words of the Roman historian Tacitus who has given us a good account of Roman activity in Wales, he 'ravaged their territory and collected extensive booty'. The pressure was only temporarily lifted when the Brigantes in the north of England rose, thus deflecting the

Roman armies. It may have been the case that Ostorius's campaign against the Deceangli was a considered strategic attempt to drive a wedge between the Brigantes and the powerful Welsh tribes, the Ordovices and the Silures.

Although Ostorius had been temporarily diverted by events in the north, it seems clear that he had decided that the heart of the British resistance now lay among the Welsh tribes. The Silures in particular were living up to their reputation for ferocity, and, as Tacitus observed, 'neither sternness nor leniency' could change their anti-Roman feelings. Moreover, the Silures were emboldened in their campaign by Caratacus who, as has been seen, had moved west after the collapse of resistance in the south-east. The Welsh tribe seems to have accepted the son of Cunobelinus as a war leader and Caratacus helped to organize resistance when, in AD 49, Ostorius invaded the land of the Silures. A legionary fortress was built to support the invasion and, although its original location is uncertain, the fortress at Usk seems eventually to have taken on this role. Excavations at Monmouth have also confirmed an early military presence on the banks of the Wye and it may be that the two great rivers helped to define the line of the Roman advance. While it is more difficult to demonstrate archaeologically, it seems likely that naval activity in the Bristol Channel would have supported the attack.

Perhaps because of the growing military pressure in south Wales, Caratacus moved with an army towards the territory of the Ordovices. He may have been attempting to link the tribes and forge a stronger anti-Roman alliance. It was a development that the Romans were determined to thwart and their armies pursued him into mid-Wales. An important and potentially decisive battle then followed. Caratacus drew his forces onto defensible high ground overlooking the Severn. The exact location of the battle continues to be a matter of debate although both Dolforwyn and Cefncarnedd have been suggested as possible sites. The early stages of the fighting were intense. Ostorius ordered his troops to cross the river and eventually, despite a shower of missiles, they were able to confront the native forces. They then formed their *testudo* (tortoise) formations, with walls and roof of locked shields, and advanced to engage on the high ground. Once that objective had been achieved, they were able to inflict a heavy defeat. The wife and daughter of Caratacus were among the many prisoners taken. Caratacus himself escaped and fled to the Brigantes but their queen Cartimandua, probably influenced by

A National Museum of Wales 'construction' of a Silurian warrior. Tacitus provides a description of the Silures, which is usually translated as tribesmen with curling hair and swarthy complexions. It is interesting, however, that Tacitus used the word coloratus *rather than the more literal* fuscus vultus, *the obvious way to say swarthy face.* Coloratus *can be translated in a number of ways; it could even refer to the Silures with their 'war-painted faces'!*

recent military activities in the north, surrendered him to the Romans.

Caratacus and his family were taken as prisoners to Rome where the recent events were regarded as a major triumph. The senate met to mark the famous day and Claudius staged a great triumphal display of his prisoners. There were, however, no fearful pleas for mercy from Caratacus whose fate would, in ordinary circumstances, have been sealed. The British war leader instead allegedly made a defiant speech to his captors. According to Tacitus, he said,

> I had horses, men, arms and wealth. Are you surprised that I am sorry to lose them? If you want to rule the world, does it follow that everyone else welcomes enslavement? If I had surrendered without a blow before being brought before you, neither my downfall nor your victory would have become famous.

The demeanour of Caratacus so impressed his captors that he and his family were spared. One of the most remarkable aspects of the episode, however, was that the loss of Caratacus seems not to have weakened the resistance of the Welsh tribes at all. In fact, the hostile Silures appear to have become even more ferocious in the aftermath of his defeat.

One reason for the hostility of the Silures was that Ostorius, perhaps with imperial authority, had said that the only solution for such a tribe was extermination or transplantation to Gaul. To support such threats, the Romans continued their programme of fort-building in the land of the Silures. The Silurian response was aggressive; a large group of Roman soldiers was cut off and surrounded. Eventually, other troops rescued them but not before the Romans had suffered heavy casualties, including the camp commandant (*praefectus castrorum*), eight centurions and a large number of men. Shortly after this victory, the Silures forced a Roman foraging party to flee to cover and then routed the cavalry that had been sent to rescue them. Only the commitment of legionary troops allowed Ostorius to regroup his forces. Continuing warfare became the order of the day along the borders of the Silures. Tacitus described the Roman discomfort reporting that 'battle followed battle'. Most of the encounters were lightning strikes in woods and bogs as the Silures adopted a highly successful guerrilla campaign. In a monument of understatement, Tacitus observed that 'the Silures were exceptionally stubborn'.

Two auxiliary cohorts, on a plundering raid, were lured into a Silurian trap and captured. The prisoners and booty were distributed among other tribes confirming the Silures as the heart of a new anti-Roman coalition. It was at this point that Ostorius died and Tacitus was clear as to the cause of his death. He was worn out by the strain of the protracted war with the Silures. For their part, the Silures 'exulted that so great a general, even if not defeated in battle, had at least been eliminated by warfare'.

The Romans moved quickly to replace Ostorius, naming Aulus Didius Gallus as the new governor. Before he arrived to take up the post, however, an even greater military disaster befell the Romans in Wales. The general Manlius Valens, presumably in an effort to claim the glory of a victory for himself before the new governor arrived, committed a legion, probably the Twentieth, against the Silures. The Silures defeated the legion! The mangled forces fell back and by the time that Didius reached Britain, he found the Silures ranging 'far and wide'. The new governor attempted to restore order in the province but he seems to have been content to maintain the *status quo* with the Welsh tribes. It was in AD 57 that hostilities resumed. A new governor, Quintus Veranius, who had made a reputation as a military leader in the Middle East, mounted a series of minor attacks against the Silures. As these were going on, however, he too died.

The next governor was Gaius Suetonius Paulinus who probably took up his new post in AD 58. Another general with a considerable reputation, Suetonius also struck into Wales. Instead of moving against the Silures, however, he marched against what seems to have been a particularly important centre of the Druids – Anglesey. Special flat-bottomed boats were built to enable the infantry to cross the Menai Straits. Many of the cavalrymen swam across beside their horses. When they landed, they were confronted by a terrifying array. Tacitus graphically describes the scene as defenders lined the shore in a dense, armed mass. With them were the Druids themselves, 'raising their hands to heaven and shouting dreadful curses', as well as 'black-robed women with dishevelled hair like Furies, brandishing torches'. At first the Romans seem to have been 'paralysed with fear', but Suetonius challenged his men not to fear a 'horde of fanatical women' and pressed the attack. As has been seen, close-quarter fighting favoured the highly disciplined Romans and they defeated the island defenders, many of whom were 'enveloped in the flames of

Boudica and Wales

Any satisfaction that Suetonius may have derived from the victory was short lived as almost immediately the province was rocked by serious rebellion. A chain of events leading to revolt began with the death of Prasutagus, client king of the Iceni. Hoping to assure the survival of his kingdom and the standing of his family, he named the emperor as his co-heir with his two daughters. This was common practice, in effect a bribe to ensure that the Roman state would enforce his will and preserve his family's position. The provincial procurator, however, responded by initiating a reign of terror among the Iceni. Boudica, the widow of Prasutagus, was flogged and her daughters were raped. The Romans then proceeded to deprive the Icenian chiefs of their hereditary estates. Not surprisingly, the Iceni, supported by other tribes such as the Trinovantes, exploded into revolt. Colchester, the former Camulodunum, Londinium and Verulamium, the modern St Albans, were sacked and burned. The Ninth legion, which had been sent to relieve Colchester, was attacked and, as Tacitus reported, 'the entire infantry force was massacred'. The intensity of the Boudican revolt was such that the expulsion of the Romans from Britain seemed a real possibility. Eventually, however, Suetonius regained control after a large set-piece battle somewhere in the Midlands. Boudica died shortly afterwards, probably having taken poison. Another suicide victim was Poenius Postumus, the temporary commander of the Second legion who had refused to move his troops from the west. This decision incensed the hard-pressed Suetonius. It is, however, at least a possibility that the decision contributed significantly to the eventual Roman victory by dissuading hostile western tribes from attempting to join the rebellion in the province. The Silures remained in Wales.

their own torches'. In the aftermath, Suetonius ordered the destruction of the sacred groves of Anglesey.

In the aftermath of the Boudican revolt, Suetonius harshly repressed the tribes in the province. His vindictive approach eventually led to his recall. The next governors, Petronius Turpilianus (AD 61–3) and Trebellius Maximus (AD 63–9), concentrated on repacification and rebuilding in the province. In

AD 67, Nero recalled the Fourteenth legion which had been based at Wroxeter and it is likely that the Twentieth legion was pulled back from Wales to replace it there. If this was the case, direct responsibility for the war with the Silures would have passed to the Second legion, then based at Exeter. This would explain the construction of a new legionary fortress at Gloucester at about this time and the shift of the Second legion to the Silurian border.

Under the emperor Nero, Rome reached a nadir of decadence which led to the end of the Julio-Claudian dynasty and to increasing military intervention in government. Particularly significant developments occurred in AD 69, the year of the four emperors, with a power struggle eventually being won by Vespasian. The new dynasty was called Flavian, after Vespasian's family name. Vespasian went on to rule for ten years during which, perhaps not surprisingly for one of the commanders in the invasion of Britain, he encouraged a more forward policy on the periphery of empire. The Romans moved back onto the offensive against the still-dangerous tribes of Wales with 'a succession of great generals' as governor, including Cerialis, Frontinus and Agricola. Central to the forward policy was Sextus Julius Frontinus who became governor in AD 73 or 74. He concentrated his attentions on subduing the Silures although, unfortunately, there are few details of his campaigns. Tacitus simply tells us that Frontinus rose 'as

An evolving symbol of power

An important discovery was made at Caerleon in the 1980s during excavations conducted by the National Museum of Wales. In the centre of the fortress, near the modern museum, footings suggested that the main streets of the fortress passed through a large tetrapylon. Surviving examples of similar structures in North Africa support towers and it may have been that the Caerleon tetrapylon could have been seen at some distance from the fortress. It would have been a strong statement of political intent as well, perhaps, as commemorating victory in the Silurian war. The Romans had come to stay! Interestingly, the excavations showed that the tetrapylon survived into the Middle Ages when it was carefully undermined. By this time, the structure may have become a very different symbol associated with Welsh kingship.

high as a man can rise' and explained that 'after a hard struggle, he conquered the powerful and warlike nation of the Silures, overcoming both the valour of his enemies and the difficulty of the terrain'. By AD 74 or 75, the Romans were secure enough in the territory of the Silures to begin building the legionary fortress at Caerleon which they called Isca.

The Second Augustan legion moved to its new permanent base on the lower Usk in the heartland of the Silures. Frontinus was also responsible for initiating construction of the legionary fortress at Chester. The resulting reorientation allowed three legions to be concentrated against the tribes of Wales. Such an overwhelming force enabled Frontinus' successor, Agricola, to embark on a policy of genocide in north Wales with an attempt to exterminate the Ordovices who had defeated a Roman cavalry unit in their territory. Many members of the tribe were killed and Agricola annexed Anglesey, the prize that Suetonius had been forced to abandon during the Boudican revolt. With this campaign, large-scale military resistance was ended in Wales. The long struggle had, however, been remarkable. The protracted guerrilla war with the Silures had presented the Romans with as intractable a problem as that posed by any other single tribe in the western empire. Given the additional hostility of the Ordovices, it is not surprising that, in AD 78, no fewer than 30,000 Roman troops were committed to Wales.

The emphasis of these troops was on consolidation of the conquest and two legions were committed to the process. The Second Augustan continued to be based at Caerleon in the south, with Second Adiutrix at Chester to control the north. In about AD 86, the Twentieth, having been withdrawn from the campaign into Scotland, replaced Second Adiutrix which was withdrawn from Britain altogether as a result of the Dacian War. Barracks, officer housing, storehouses and other timber-frame buildings were built in AD 74-5 at Caerleon, in the heartland of the Silures. The site, with its convenient access to supplies by land and sea, was probably seen as a permanent one from the outset and within a decade or two buildings were rebuilt in stone. By the end of the first century, an imposing 1.5m-thick stone wall with turrets and stone gateways had replaced the early wooden defences. Internal structures such as the tribune's house, which partially underlies the modern museum, were also converted to stone. Some buildings were of masonry construction from the outset; notable among them was the large and elaborate fortress baths building. Another important early construction was the amphitheatre, an elliptical arena surrounded by a grandstand which could provide seating for some 5–6,000 men – the entire complement of the legion.

Many Roman military sites have been found in Wales and it is reasonable to assume that still others await discovery. Some sites were occupied for only a short period of time. There are, for example, marching camps and large vexillation fortresses, covering up to twenty acres, which were built as temporary strongholds by battle groups on campaign. There are also interesting constructions like the special practice camps which consisted solely of corners and entrances probably intended only for training in construction techniques and for target practice by troops using *ballistae* and other siege machines. Earthworks on Llandrindod Wells Common provide an interesting example. Particularly important in the military occupation of Wales were a number of permanent forts to accommodate auxiliary troops who were charged with patrolling the still potentially hostile Welsh countryside. A network of forts, accommodating units of between 500 and 1,000 men, extended across the length and breadth of Wales. Excavation of some of these forts has provided interesting insights into the military occupation. A tombstone at Brecon Gaer, for example, informs us that a Spanish cavalry regiment, Ala Hispanorum Vettonum, once occupied that fort. Spanish troops also seem to have been assigned to the fort at Llanio in Dyfed. Inscriptions suggest that Celtic auxiliaries, the Belgic Nervians, were once at Caer-gai in Gwynedd. It has been argued that because of the proximity of the Roman gold mines at Dolaucothi, legionary troops may have been assigned to the fort at Pumsaint in Dyfed. By about AD 80, a network of forts dominated the whole of Wales and continued to do so for nearly half a century. There then followed a period of consolidation, in part because units were withdrawn for service in other regions such as the area near Hadrian's Wall. Those at the most strategically significant locations, however, were maintained for centuries.

This network of Roman military sites not only provided a framework for control, it also provided a mechanism for the intro-duction of *romanitas*; cultural as well as military imperialism was implicit in the newly imposed structures of society. There were, for example, fundamental changes in the management of resources which went beyond the imposition of a 'money economy'. An important innovation was the creation of towns, with important urban centres such as Cowbridge (Bovium) emerging, presumably as a market centre for the Vale of Glamorgan where, as will be seen, a villa economy was developing. Cowbridge probably grew as a 'ribbon development' with buildings concentrated along the road, roughly approximating to the line of today's high-street shops. Roof tiles stamped LEG II AUG suggest some sort of association with the Second Augustan legion which may have been responsible for construction of the excavated bath-house in the town. Other small towns may have developed from *vici*, settlements which grew up around forts at sites like Caerhun in Gwynedd and Trawsgoed in Dyfed. Some sites seem to have had a largely industrial function; Abergavenny (Gobannium) and Monmouth (Blestium) in Gwent are both cases in point

Romanitas and the Silures: the creation of a civitas

One of the most important steps in the imposition of *romanitas* was the creation of *civitas* administration. The *civitates* were units of local administration based on the tribe. Two were created in Wales; one in the territory of the Silures and the other in the land of the Demetae. Each of these units would have had a *civitas* capital to function as an administrative centre for local government. The capital of the Demetae was Carmarthen, Moridunum Demetarum. Despite its status, Carmarthen remained a small urban centre perhaps extending only to about fifteen acres. There

Dating the civitas

The excavations generated particular interest since dating the basilica would give a good indication of when the *civitas* was established. Some authorities had argued that *civitas* administration came early as an initiative of Frontinus. Others argued that, given the intensity of the protracted war with the Silures, a long period of pacification would have been required before any such devolution of authority would have taken place. Archaeology has now clarified the situation; dating evidence for the construction levels of the basilica suggests that it was a Hadrianic building. Construction in the 120s is important as it is known that troops including members of the Second Augustan legion were moved from Wales to assist in construction of the wall at that time. Moreover, a gap of half a century since the conquest would have allowed time for a gradual improvement of relationships between the Romans and the Silures.

are a number of open questions about both the foundation and the operation of the town. The most fully excavated feature is the amphitheatre which was cut into a hillside with the dug-out soil used to make an outer seating bank. The amphitheatre was large with dimensions of 91m by 67m and it has been suggested that it could have served as a tribal gathering place. Turf and clay defences surrounded the town and limited excavations suggest that contained within the walls were houses, shops and workshops. At least one of the houses was warmed by a hypocaust.

An interpretation of the forum and basilica at Caerwent. The dress of the inhabitants, ranging from Roman to native, suggests conflation of culture in the civitas *capital.*

With the exception of the large civil settlement which grew up around Caerleon, the largest urban centre in Roman Wales was Caerwent, Venta Silurum, the *civitas* capital of the Silures. A site of approximately forty-four acres, the town had early defences of earthen banks and ditches which were later replaced by substantial stone walls and well-defended gates. The town was divided in half by a main 'high street' which ran from east to west. A number of shops faced onto this street which was flanked by two other parallel streets. Four streets then ran from north to south, dividing the town into twenty blocks or *insulae*. The central *insulae* contained the main public buildings including the forum and the basilica which have recently been excavated by Richard Brewer and a team from the National Museum of Wales. Among findings in the basilica is the senate chamber where the *ordo* of the Silures met.

In the fullness of time, Caerwent became a thriving urban centre; at its peak some 2–3,000 people lived in the town. It seems reasonable to assume that the town would have been an important influence in transmitting *romanitas* to the local population. As will be seen, artefacts with religious associations clearly demonstrate conflation of culture. The same can be said for a carved stone pedestal which survives from Caerwent. According to the inscription, the monument was erected to honour Tiberius Claudius Paulinus in about AD 220. It was raised by *respublica civitatis Silurum,* erected by decree and authority of the tribal senate of the Silures. The existence of the senate confirms Roman administrative practices in the early third century; it also confirms the survival of the tribal identity in the *civitas.* As will be seen, that tribal identity and associated native traditions may have remained surprisingly strong even within the *civitas* capital.

Rural settlement after the Roman conquest

It has become something of a cliché to emphasize the differences in levels of romanization between south-east Wales and the rest of the region. But while such a model has to be modified in the light of an ever-increasing body of archaeological evidence, it remains broadly the case that the highest levels of Roman civilization manifest themselves around the *civitas* capital of Caerwent and in the Vale of Glamorgan. By the early second century AD, when Wales was largely free of a military presence (most forces having been deployed to northern Britain), the benefits of the *pax romana* enabled the Silurian population to tap into the new market economy and manifested themselves in the opportunity for the local gentry to invest their prosperity in Roman-style dwellings, with all the trappings of 'civilization': heated bath-houses, painted wall-plaster and mosaic pavements. Whilst it is possible to identify the generation of increasing wealth and the use of Roman goods elsewhere in Wales, there is nothing to compare with the well-organized, essentially romanized farming system that pertained in the south-east.

A striking feature of rural Wales in the Roman period (including the relatively romanized south-east) is the pattern of reoccupation of settlement sites from the Iron Age into the post-conquest era. Time and again, archaeological investigation reveals that a house of Roman date was preceded by an Iron Age dwelling. Sometimes the sequence suggests direct continuity; in other cases, a dislocation in settlement is indicated with, perhaps, a considerable gap between one period of occupation and the next. It is clear that the Romano-British settlement pattern in rural Wales is closely linked – both in terms of character and extent – to that of Iron Age occupation. The reuse of Iron Age sites in the Roman period occurred not only in lowland areas but even on land occupied by Iron Age hillforts. Dinorben in the north and Castell Henllys in the south-west exemplify this phenomenon. Overall, the pattern of rural settlement in the Roman period is strongly indicative of relatively static communities which, whether they fully embraced and benefited from the new Roman ways or remained largely unaffected by the intrusive culture, were certainly not subjected to significant upheaval in their landownership after the conquest. It is also very evident that Wales, like the rest of Britain, continued to support considerable regional diversity in the manner in which land was settled and exploited.

The south-east

The area of Wales occupied by the Silures itself exhibits a wide range of rural homesteads, from the villas of prosperous landowners to the smallholdings of subsistence (or tenant) farmers with minimal signs of *romanitas*. But it should be stressed that all these habitations – the vast majority of which were farms – were occupied by Britons, the descendants of Iron Age communities.

During the Roman period, the British aristocracy of the south-east arguably exchanged the old Iron Age Celtic signs of status – the possession of rich metalwork and military equipment – for a new 'language' of wealth and rank: the outward and visible adoption of *romanitas*. Some landowners exhibited a wholly romanized lifestyle by building grandiose villas in the Roman manner: the country estates at Ely, Llantwit Major and Llandough exemplify this new tradition. Of the villas excavated in this region, Ely appears to be unique inasmuch as it seems to have been newly established in the Roman period, perhaps in response to a growing need for an economic surplus in the production and marketing of foodstuffs. The main house, built in the second century AD, was of winged-corridor type, with a west range occupied by a bath-suite. The house possessed central heating and

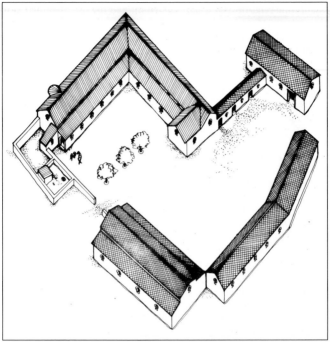

Reconstruction drawing of the Roman courtyard villa at Llantwit Major, Glamorgan, the residence of a well-to-do Romano-Briton but, none the less, a working farm. The owners lived in the main house (top of picture); there were other ranges of rooms, including one probably inhabited by farmworkers.

tessellated floors, and underwent modifications until an apparent cessation of occupation in the mid-fourth century AD.

Llantwit Major and Llandough were substantive villas, like Ely, but both sites were occupied by earlier establishments of Iron Age date. Llantwit was a courtyard villa with separate ranges of living quarters for the owner's family and for servants. Baths, hypocausts and mosaics bear witness to a comfortable, prosperous lifestyle. Storage and workshop facilities are testimony to the functional, working aspect of villa life. It has been suggested that Llantwit was the centre of a main land-managing estate that may have supported tenant farmers, on sites like Biglis nearby, in a symbiotic relationship where the tenant had the use of rented land in exchange for the provision of goods and services to the main villa. Such a pattern of reciprocity gains credence from the lack of accommodation at Llantwit itself for large numbers of estate workers. Unlike Ely (and other prosperous farms, such as Llandough and the less romanized house at Whitton), Llantwit Major evidently underwent a decline during the third century AD, but enjoyed a revival in the late third/early fourth century. The villa appears to have been abandoned in the later fourth century.

A Silurian farm

The farmers inhabiting Whitton lived in an essentially indigenous style of house until romanizing architecture was adopted in the late first or early second century AD. The first phase of occupation consisted of a sub-rectangular ditched enclosure, with a strongly defended entrance-way, containing a series of small roundhouses, perhaps belonging to an extended family. The economy here was based on pastoral farming, particularly the raising of sheep and pigs for wool and meat. Deer were hunted, shellfish gathered and arable land farmed. T-shaped furnaces were used for drying corn, malting barley for beer and/or smoking or drying fish. The community smelted and forged iron, probably for home consumption. Prosperity is indicated by the presence of manufactured goods, such as imported pottery, glass and bronze objects; these must have been paid for by surplus production from the farm. The bronze steelyard and iron *styli* found on the site suggest that accounts were kept. Although the inhabitants of Whitton adopted romanized architectural traditions, the family enjoyed a less lavish lifestyle than the occupiers of Ely or Llantwit. A limited amount of decorated plaster adorned the walls and, although two hypocausts were built, they were never fired, and no traces of mosaic floors were found.

The villa at Llandough, near Cardiff, had a long and complex history. It began in the late Iron Age with a circular farmhouse and an agricultural economy, supplemented by exploitation of the natural resources from the nearby sea and local rivers. Early in the second century AD, the round timber-house was replaced by a romanized dwelling, with a rectangular ground-plan and stone foundations, a hypocaust heating system, painted plaster on the walls and tessellated floors. The growing economic prosperity of this romanized farming family is exhibited by expansion in the third century, when the size of the establishment was increased by an additional range of rooms and a new bath-suite. Like most Romano-British settlements in the region, the Llandough villa declined in the mid-fourth century. But later, the site was the focus for a major early Christian monastic cemetery, which had its genesis in the late Roman period.

The villas at Ely, Llantwit and Llandough represent the pinnacle of overt rural romanization in south-east Wales. Further down the scale, but still evincing signs of considerable prosperity within the Roman market economy, were establishments like Whitton and Caldicot. Excavations at Whitton revealed an unbroken sequence of occupation from *c.* AD 30 until the mid-fourth century AD. There is thus no evidence for the occupation of the site until a decade or so before the Roman conquest.

Caldicot, only a kilometre from Caerwent, was of similar status to Whitton but – as one of several 'satellite' settlements around the Silurian capital – its fortunes were inextricably tied to that of the urban community. Like Whitton, Caldicot began life in the later Iron Age and enjoyed an increasing level of romanization in the early second century, the improved standards of living supported by continued exploitation of the fertile soil around the Severn estuary.

Other farms in Silurian territory exhibit a relatively low level of romanization, which probably reflects either a subsistence economy (with no available surplus to pay for new buildings or lavish furnishings) or tenant-farmer status. The latter is suggested as pertaining to Biglis, which was inhabited both pre- and post-conquest, but with a break in occupation at the end of the first century AD. The farm was supported by a mixed economy, including hunting and stock-rearing. Although occupation continued here until the mid-fourth century, Biglis displays little romanization in its long history. A similar pattern can be observed at other sites, like Cae Summerhouse, where timber was still the building material used in the mid-fourth century. Although the settlement at Mynydd Bychan was enclosed by drystone walls, the owners lived in circular timber-houses until the abandonment of the farm early in the second century AD (before it had a chance to develop any potential for prosperity).

Excavations at Thornwell Farm, Chepstow have revealed traces of repeated occupation of the site, which began life as a single circular high-status building in the late Bronze Age/early Iron Age transition period. Occupation in the late Iron Age took a different form, with a series of smaller dwellings set within a walled enclosure; the settlement was then continuously inhabited throughout the Roman period, with no apparent dislocation caused by the conquest. In these phases, the family/community at Thornwell presumably subsisted on a mixed economy, including cultivation and stock-rearing: the animal-bones reveal a bias in favour of sheep or goats. At least six infants were buried in pits on the site. Evidence from pottery suggests that, in common with other farms in the region, the site was either abandoned in the mid-fourth century or was, at least, aceramic after that date.

The south-west

If south-east Wales reveals evidence for widely contrasting levels of romanization among the indigenous population, the south-west as a whole (the territory of the Demetae) seems to have been far less influenced by Roman lifestyles or material culture, probably because the communities here were generally further away from established Roman markets. Iron Age society appears to have continued into the Roman period with little change, although some rural homesteads demonstrate a thin veneer of romanization. Interestingly, there is some evidence for a hierarchy of settlement but – unlike the situation among the Silures – status and *romanitas* did not necessarily go hand in hand. The overall paucity of artefacts from these sites inhibits both chronological and functional interpretation by archaeologists, but it is possible to identify a pattern of settlement wherein good agricultural land was occupied, despite the absence of good immediate water supplies.

An important group of sites occupied both pre- and post-conquest – though with little overt sign of direct continuity of settlement – consists of the raths or 'ring-forts', built in the Iron Age and sometimes resettled in Roman times. Walesland (occupied between the first century BC and the third century AD) and Coygan Camp are examples of these homesteads, which lay within disused later Iron Age defences. Another one – at Trelissey – has been interpreted as a high-status structure that may have had a ceremonial or political function rather than that of a simple farm. Romano-British occupation, in the second–third centuries AD, was concentrated in an annexe of a small Iron Age hillfort at

Castell Henllys, Nevern, though the main enclosure had apparently been deserted.

Some defended farmsteads seem not to have been established until after the Roman conquest. The cluster of sites at Llawhaden, consisting of a mixture of roundhouses and four-post structures, has revealed pottery dating to the first and second centuries AD. Later in the Roman period, some more romanized farms developed here. Thus, at Dan-y-coed, the earlier farm was transformed into an undefended dwelling, with a rectangular form and a sunken yard. It is significant that the more easterly farms, which fell within the market network focused on the Roman town of Carmarthen, exhibit something akin to 'villa' status. It was this area – the Tywi Valley – whose large Iron Age hillforts display the most signs of pre-Roman wealth, and it is likely that the descendants of the local 'Celtic' lords who had built the hillforts occupied these relatively prosperous romanized farms.

So communities of the Demetae reacted differentially to the opportunities offered by *romanitas*. The adoption of rectangularity at Dan-y-coed may have been influenced by the new architectural tradition but, at Walesland, for instance, roundhouses were maintained until late in the Roman period. Some families, at least, engaged in external trade: non-local Roman pottery was used, for example, at Llawhaden and Castell Henllys. Compared with south-east Wales, society in the south-west seems to have been seldom disturbed by the Roman presence, and some families managed to ignore it almost completely.

The north-east

In the north-east the romanization of the local population is most evident in areas impinged upon by the activities of the Twentieth legion, which was based at Chester. Thus the stone buildings at Ffrith, associated with Roman military material and some fine pottery, may represent an army posting-station rather than a farm. Another lowland site, a farmstead with adjacent field-systems at Rhuddlan, remained firmly native throughout the Roman period: a roundhouse associated with another – possibly rectangular – timber structure was erected in the later first century AD, but most activity seems to have taken place at least two centuries later. In the later Iron Age, a small farm was built at Prestatyn dated (by C14) to the second–first century BC. Archaeological investigation revealed traces of a roundhouse, an animal pen and an infant burial. Between the later first and earlier second century AD the site appears to have developed into an industrial establishment, with bronze workshops and a bath-house, based around a probable harbour. The inference is that the settlement expanded during the second century in response to a reorganization of local mining, associated with support from the legionary works depot at Holt.

Dinorben perhaps represents the most interesting aspect of Romano-British settlement in north-east Wales. The final refurbishment of the hillfort ramparts took place in response to the advance of the Roman army in the late first century AD. There followed a long period of abandonment until the site was resettled, as an undefended dwelling. The new building, erected in the third century AD (according to the evidence of abundant bronze coin deposition) was a large timber roundhouse, apparently owned by a member of the local nobility who adopted some trappings of Roman culture but whose rank related to his role in indigenous society: outward signs of his local status included ceremonial accoutrements such as a sceptre and a decorated bucket.

The north-west

The surviving traces of settlement in Gwynedd reveal a variety of rural dwellings of which some were occupied both before and during the Roman period. Certain buildings consisted of multiple or compartmentalized structures, built of drystone, some roofed, others open. Unlike others of this type, the settlement at Din Lligwy was established only after the Roman conquest, in the second century AD, lasting at least until the fifth century. The entrance-way, with its massive gate-house, led to a building with a complex ground-plan of open stock-pens or working areas and roofed living space; it probably housed a single family of between five and ten people. The complex at Din Lligwy was associated with terraced fields; the presence of querns and mortars, together with large numbers of animal-bones (mainly of cattle and sheep), attest to the mixed economy supporting the farmstead. Some metalworking also took place on the site. The relative prosperity and romanization of the settlement is indicated by the several hundred potsherds found here, including imported wares, glass and Roman coins. Din Lligwy has been identified as a north-western equivalent of the rich villas of the south-east.

Some rural farms were occupied over a long time span; two sites exemplify this pattern of longevity: Graeanog and Bryn Eryr. Graeanog was inhabited from the late first millennium BC until the fourth century AD. The initial phase of construction comprised two

Wrought-iron fire-dog (a piece of hearth-furniture) from Capel Garmon, Gwynedd; first century AD. The fire-dog is superbly ornamented with maned bulls' heads; it involved complex technology and craftsmanship, possibly taking as long as three person-years to produce. It would have been a highly prized, prestigious object to own. Ht. 75cm.

Bronze plaque ornamented in repoussé with a 'broken-backed' (or angled) triskele design; from Moel Hiraddug, Clwyd. The triskele is common in Welsh Iron Age art, and was probably a symbolic motif. The plate may once have decorated a box or shield. Length of each side 16.3cm.

Reconstruction painting of ritual activity at the sacred lake of Llyn Fawr, Glamorgan, where two great cauldrons, other bronzes and some of the earliest iron objects known from Wales were deliberately deposited, as gifts to the gods, in the seventh century BC. The painting shows people gathering at the lakeside and casting the metalwork into the water.

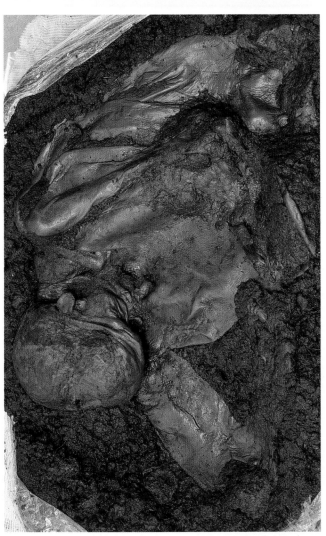

Lindow Man, a bog-body from Lindow Moss, Cheshire. Dating to the mid-first century AD, this young man may have been a human sacrifice, ritually killed at a time of great crisis in the community. He suffered two violent blows to the head, was garotted and had his throat cut before being thrust face down, naked, into a pool in the marsh.

Part of an enamelled bronze bowl-handle, in the form of a cat's face, from Snowdon, Gwynedd; first century AD. The design is deceptively simple but effective and demonstrates the consummate skill of the metalsmith. The earliest faunal evidence for domestic cats in Britain is the late Iron Age. Width of cat's face 2.5cm.

Crescentric bronze plaque decorated with a triskele whose arms terminate in birds' heads. From the ritual deposit at Llyn Cerrig Bach, Anglesey; first century AD. The piece probably once adorned an item of war-gear, perhaps a chariot (several chariot-fragments, including iron tyres, were found in the same hoard).

Stone statuette of a seated goddess, found in a well at the Romano-British town of Caerwent, tribal capital of the Silures; second century AD. The goddess appears to be hooded; she holds a circular object, perhaps an apple, and a tree or palm-branch. Her deposition deep underground may be significant and she may have represented a divine earth-mother.

Bronze bucket-escutcheon in the form of a bull's head, from Dinorben, Gwynedd. First century AD. It once decorated a sheet-bronze vessel that probably belonged to a high-ranking individual, and was used at feasts. The bull-motif would have been appropriate since cattle were considered as units of wealth in early British and Irish society.

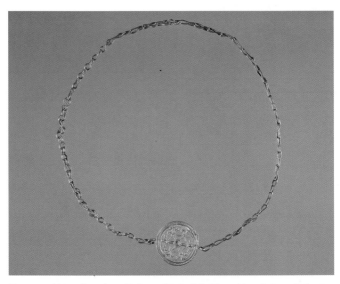

Roman gold jewellery from Dolaucothi, Dyfed. The golden chain and wheel-pendant may have been made near the gold-mine site. Ornaments like this have been found elsewhere in Britain and throughout the Roman empire.

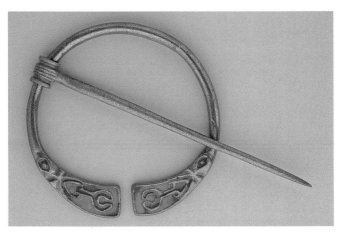

A reconstructed enamelled zoomorphic penannular brooch based on a terminal excavated at Dinas Powys. The pin is based on early medieval parallels from Ireland.

The cross erected by Hywel ap Rhys, who ruled Glywysing until his death in AD 886. The inscription says in part, 'Hywel prepared this cross for the soul of Rhys his father.'

Stylised bronze boar-figurine from a cave at Rhossili, Gower (it has no exact provenance); Iron Age or Roman date. Max. length 5.7cm.

Gold bowl, decorated with animals, including deer and a hare; above is a frieze of alternating full and new moons (or crescent moons and suns); from Altstetten, Zürich; sixth century BC. The symbolism on this vessel may relate to seasonality and the passing of time: the celestial motifs would fit such an interpretation, and the presence of antlers on some deer but not others may reflect the annual growth and shedding of antlers on stags (unless it relates to different genders). Diameter 25cm.

large unenclosed stone roundhouses; this plan underwent modification, presumably because of Roman influence, and developed into an enclosed smallholding with rectangular buildings. The owners imported Roman pottery, including samian ware. The soil was too acid for animal-bones to survive but spindle-whorls indicate that wool was woven, and there was evidence also for subsistence metalworking. Interestingly, after a hiatus in occupation, Graeanog was resettled in the medieval period. Bryn Eryr was similarly inhabited during the later Iron Age and Roman period, until the third century AD, apparently continuously, although lacking evidence for medieval occupation (see chapter 2).

Religious life

When the Romans occupied Britain, they brought with them both the 'iconographic habit' and the 'epigraphic habit', along with the tradition of venerating the supernatural forces in sacred buildings – temples – which conformed to a formalized architectural convention, marking them out as unequivocally associated with religion and ritual. Although the pre-Roman Britons (and their nearest neighbours in Gaul) did sometimes fashion images of their gods in wood and, occasionally, in stone, there is no doubt that the Roman occupation of these lands resulted in a vast increase in this kind of tangible acknowledgement of a spirit-world inhabited by deities who were perceived as more or less resembling humans. Alongside this developed tradition of depicting divine images, the Romans introduced the idea of setting up inscribed dedications which, for the first time, identified gods and goddesses by name. It may be that such formalization of the supernatural world, involving codification of divine identity by means of depiction and nomenclature in the permanence of stone, actually influenced the manner in which the gods were perceived and venerated. It may also be that the huge range of sacred images, with no apparent Iron Age forebears, that appeared in Britain and Gaul during the Roman period represented a deliberate invention of a new Gallo-British pantheon, as a reaction to the introduction of intrusive Roman cults and in a vigorous reassertion of 'Celtic' identity. This may account for the presence of god-forms – like those of Epona and Hammer-God – who, though apparently worshipped and depicted for the first time after the Roman conquest, bore little resemblance to any members of the Graeco-Roman pantheon.

Deities

The Roman army brought their gods with them to Wales. Jupiter, Fortuna, Mercury and other divinities originating from Italy were venerated, for instance, at Caerleon. Alongside divinities of Mediterranean origin, the troops introduced the more exotic cult of Mithras, a saviour-god of Persian origin, and *mithraea* are known to have been established at Caerleon and Segontium. But it is interesting to observe that – even in Roman military installations – there is evidence for the worship of deities that were either indigenous to Britain or, more likely, were imported from Gaul. Soldiers took care to pay homage not only to the state-gods of Rome but also to the spirits of their homeland and of the new territory they were occupying. Some of the antefixes (triangular clay tiles that fitted onto the gable-ends of roofs) found at Caerleon were adorned with human faces accompanied by celestial symbols, including solar wheels. From archaeological evidence, it is possible to identify a Gallo-British celestial god whose emblem was a spoked wheel and who was venerated throughout western Europe in both pre-Roman and Roman periods. It is noteworthy, too, that another Gaulish sky-god, a thunderer named Taranis, was worshipped in the legionary fortress at Chester.

The few images of divinities that are probably of Iron Age date (see chapter 2, p. 31) are devoid of specific symbolism, thus making it impossible to link the iconography with any functional identification. Indeed, in the absence of secure archaeological contexts for such 'featureless' images, it may be difficult to ascribe them even to the pre- or post-conquest period with any confidence. This is true, for instance, of the curious 'cult-pillar' carved with a schematic human face, which was found built into a modern wall in Port Talbot. The face has parallels in Romano-British sculpture, like the stone head from Eype in Dorset and some of the many carved heads from northern Britain, but it is equally reminiscent of heads dating to the Iron Age, such as those incised on the 'head-pillar' from Entremont in southern Gaul. Another stone head from Wales, however, has a definite Roman context; it was found on a platform in what may have been a shrine-chamber in the remotest part of grounds belonging to a late Roman house at Caerwent. Heads like these may represent specific gods whose identity is unknown but, alternatively, they could have possessed a talismanic function: there is archaeological evidence for the special treatment accorded human skulls at, for instance, the Iron Age hillfort of Danebury and in the pre-Roman sanctuaries at Roquepertuse and Entremont, in the Lower Rhône Valley; Graeco-Roman writers of the first century BC/first century AD – such as Strabo and Diodorus Siculus – allude to the value of decapitated enemy heads as sacred trophies among the Gauls.

Image of a native British warrior-god, incised on a pebble from Tre Owen, Newtown, Powys. He carries a sword and shield; by his side is an animal, probably a dog. Max. width 19.5cm.

Some Gallo-British divinities from Roman Wales can be identified in terms of function and, occasionally, by name. The stone statuette of a seated goddess from the vicinity of the temple adjacent to the forum-basilica at Caerwent is probably that of a mother-goddess, one of many depictions from Britain and Gaul. The *Deae Matres* were frequently portrayed in threes: there are several examples of triadic female images from Cirencester, for instance. But 'single' mother-goddesses are not uncommon: one from Cirencester holds three apples in her lap, and a similar image, with a basket of fruit on her knees, comes from Alesia in central Gaul. The Caerwent goddess also bears a piece of fruit, a common emblem of abundance, and a second motif which has been interpreted as a palm-branch, a conifer or an ear of corn (maybe

A local Mars at Caerwent

Two inscriptions from Caerwent bear witness to the veneration of a single (or two related) Celtic divinities whose names and identities were conflated with the Roman Mars. One consists of a stone altar dedicated to Mars Ocelus; the second is the base of a statue set up to 'Mars Lenus or Ocelus Vellaunus', by Marcus Nonius Romanus in AD 152. Lenus Mars was a healer-god of the Treveri in the Moselle Valley, and temples to him were set up at their *civitas* capital Augusta Treverorum (Trier) and in the neighbouring countryside. Nonus Romanus was perhaps himself an expatriot Treveran. In Britain, Lenus was also venerated at the Roman villa of Chedworth in Gloucestershire. Vellaunus' name only occurs outside Caerwent among the Allobroges of southern Gaul, whilst Ocelus seems to have been a British god, worshipped at Carlisle. The only surviving part of the statue of Lenus are a pair of human feet and the webbed feet of a goose, a particular symbol of Gallo-British versions of Mars, presumably because of its reputation for alertness and aggressive protection. In Gaul and Britain, the symbolism of Mars was frequently altered from that of war to combat against disease or barrenness.

all three), all of which may relate to symbolism associated with fecundity, regeneration or victory. Interestingly, the context of the Caerwent goddess, near the bottom of a deep pit, is strongly reminiscent of the findspot for the Alesia statue, which had been placed in a subterranean cellar beneath a house. This underground position may reflect a chthonic or netherworld dimension to the Celtic mother-goddess cult.

A lost image, roughly incised on a large round pebble from Tre Owen, Newtown in Powys, is also of Roman date, and is associated with pottery of the third century AD. The figure is that of a warrior, naked but for a wreath, and bearing a sword and a circular shield; an altar is depicted beneath his right arm, and standing by his right leg is a dog-like animal; crudely scratched letters suggest that the image represents a native version of Mars. It may be significant that, like the Caerwent goddess, this image comes from the base of a pit or well.

Sacred places

In Gaul and Britain, the most frequent form of temple-building is the so-called 'Romano-Celtic' type, consisting of an inner *cella* surrounded by a concentric portico (of rectilinear, circular or polygonal shape), the whole set within a *temenos* (sacred enclosure). The relative thickness of the walls suggests that the *cella* stood higher than the ambulatory. The distribution of these temples in western Europe indicates a non-Mediterranean origin for the form, and the architecture appears to have developed as a blend of Classical and Gallo-British traditions. The best evidence for the presence of this type of temple in Wales comes from Caerwent, where a stone-founded sanctuary, with an apsidal *cella* was built next to the forum-basilica in the later third century AD. The presence of a preceding shrine on the site is suggested by traces of an earlier stone structure. The identity of the divinity worshipped at the Caerwent temple is unknown.

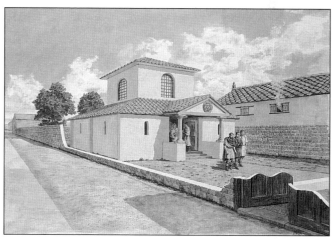

Reconstruction of the Romano-Celtic temple at Caerwent, with its tall inner cella *and surrounding portico. The shrine was built in the third century AD, next to the forum-basilica.*

Sanctuaries elsewhere in Wales have been revealed by air photography or by scatters of surface finds. Temple-sites at Gwehelog, near Usk in the south-east, and in the north-east, near Ruthin in the Vale of Clwyd have shown up during aerial reconnaissance.

67

The latter shrine is revealed as a rectilinear ditched enclosure bounded by double walls, with internal colonnades; inside are faint traces of a temple-building. At Gwehelog, a circular shrine was placed off-centre within a rectangular-walled precinct; the air photographs picked up traces of an earlier round building and, if this is correctly interpreted, the Gwehelog site may reflect the presence of a native shrine (built on the same pattern as Iron Age roundhouses) which was later restructured according to more romanized conventions. Finally, an important temple may have existed at Llys Awel, near Abergele in Clwyd, where metal-detector activity has discovered a number of finds including several late Roman coin-hoards, a figurine of Mercury and some small images of dogs, reminiscent of the offerings made to the British healer-god Nodens at the major sanctuary of Lydney, on the Severn.

4 The First Christians in Wales

Later Roman Britain: the growth of industry

The large villas in the south-east of Wales which show clear indications of the adoption of *romanitas* suggest both prosperity and an accommodation, at least by some members of the British aristocracy, with Roman custom and practice. Growing towns, expanding trade and increasingly more efficient farming indicate that Roman Britain, including Wales, seems to have prospered in the second and third centuries. Industrial development was important in helping to provide a foundation for this new prosperity and, particularly in the early years, the extractive industries were important. This is not surprising since, from the outset, the Romans were intent on exploiting the resources of their newly conquered lands to the full and, as has been seen, Britain was known to have large reserves of several valuable metals. Significantly, many of these reserves were in Wales which became a centre of Roman mining. Mines were generally let by a procurator of mines to concessionaires (*conductores*) and some, like C. Nipius Ascanius, seem to have extended their activities into areas beyond Roman military control at a very early date. He was, for example, acquiring lead in Clwyd as early as AD 60 and pigs of lead stamped as Deceanglian may have been produced to be traded to the Romans.

Among the most sought-after metals in Wales were copper and zinc which were available at sites in north and mid-Wales including Parys Mountain on Anglesey, the Great Orme in Gwynedd and Llanymynech Hill in Powys. Deposits of lead, which had a number of uses ranging from water pipes to coffins, were found in west Wales, Glamorgan and Gwent as well as in the north-east. One particularly important use for lead was in production of pewter, and the fact that silver was often present in lead deposits made it highly valued. Gold was another much-valued metal, and the gold mine at Dolaucothi was one of the most interesting mining initiatives in Wales. This unique British example of a Roman gold mine, which may have begun in the pre-Roman period, developed into a large-scale operation with an aqueduct system, opencast workings and impressive hand-cut adits. The adits gave access to large galleries and, in one of these, fragments of a timber waterwheel have been found. Radiocarbon dating has established that the wheel was Roman and suggests that mining at Dolaucothi applied principles developed on the Continent. The Romans are known to have constructed elaborate systems to harness water power and both Diodorus Siculus and Pliny describe Spanish mines where large waterwheels were used to drain underground galleries upward from one level to another. A similar system seems to have been in use at Dolaucothi where hydraulic technology was also employed outside the mine with aqueducts creating water courses for use in hushing, a process where a rush of water scoured topsoil to expose ore-bearing rock, and in washing ore to separate the gold. Additional isolated tanks were probably used in 'quenching' after fire-setting, a technique in which fires were used to heat and crack the rock in order to expose the ore.

Welsh gold

It is likely that while contractors conducted the mining operations at Dolaucothi, the army had an active role in protecting gold shipments. A fort was built at Pumsaint near the gold mines and there is evidence that eventually a *vicus* developed near the fort. Among the most interesting finds from Dolaucothi are a number of examples of gold jewellery, some of which were fashioned into distinctive snake-shaped bracelets, brooches and other ornaments. These finds represent good evidence that goldsmiths were actually working on or near the gold-mine site, producing items of very high quality.

As has been noted, copper continued to be extracted in Wales. At the mine at Llanymynech Hill, a ramp was made to give access into the mine which, in addition to adits for prospecting, consisted of a main gallery where miners followed the lode for some distance. Several died in doing so and were buried in the galleries. Larger copper mines were sunk at the Great Orme and Parys Mountain which was probably the largest mining operation in Wales. An important mining site in the south-east is the Roman lead mine at Draethen in Gwent. Here the system extended for some 120m underground with a large entrance-chamber connected by a passage leading into a gallery. What makes the site a particularly interesting one, however, is that there is evidence that the interests of the operators of the mine went beyond simply extracting lead. Finds from Draethen imply that in the third century a counterfeiting operation was being conducted on the site.

Another significant element in the Romano-British economy was the iron industry which in the early years may, in a civilian context, have drawn from existing native practices. As has been seen (pp. 20–1), iron-working was important in pre-conquest society with particularly important sites in north Wales such as Crawcwellt West and Bryn y Castell which demonstrate efficient production systems and the smelting of bog ore. As the Romano-British economy grew, however, the scale of production and methods of extraction developed rapidly. It is known that one important source of ore was the Forest of Dean and that Dean ores were smelted on sites in south-east Wales. Ore may also have been mined in Glamorgan and Gwent and the Roman name for Abergavenny, Gobannium, may derive from iron-working there. The key element in the name is *gobann* which seems to be related to *gof* or smith in modern Welsh. If this interpretation is correct, the name may suggest iron-working before the establishment of the early fort; whether this was the case or not, smithing certainly seems to have been important during the Roman period, as was the case at nearby Usk. Britain had become self-sufficient in iron production by the end of the first century and emerged as a substantial iron exporter to regions like Gaul and the Rhineland in the second century and after. There are indications that there was a general decline in the industry in the mid-fourth century but even then local demand continued to be high. Consequently, there continued to be a number of small-scale producers in both the towns and villas of later Roman Britain. The late iron-working activity at the Pound Lane site in Caerwent is a case in point.

The Romano-British economy was not, of course, solely dependent on heavy industry and mining. As Roman traditions became more widely accepted, specialized local industries developed to cater for changing tastes. An obvious example is the production of mosaics; groups of craftsmen formed firms and used common pattern-books to lay pavements in towns and villas. Another important industry was textile production and, by the fourth century, many villas were given over to sheep production to supply the necessary wool. There was a demand for British textiles on the Continent and items produced for export included a sort of

Fine wines and British beers

A range of export goods was reflected in demands for imports and, not surprisingly given the strength of the pre-conquest wine trade, wine was important in the system of trade. Cargoes of amphorae brought wine from Italy, Spain and the Rhineland as well as from some of the still famous wine-producing areas of Gaul including Bordeaux, the Gironde, Moselle and the Champagne region. Interestingly, there is evidence that wines were produced in other regions which are not major wine-producing districts today. Production in areas such as the upland reaches of the Dordogne probably indicates subsequent climate changes. While there is no direct evidence for wine production in Roman Wales, there is a suggestion of Roman vineyards in places like Gloucester although it is impossible to quantify British wine production on the basis of presently available evidence. Whatever the nature of local production, however, the majority of wine consumed was imported and cargoes of amphorae brought significant quantities into places like Caerleon. It is important to remember that not all of the cargoes of amphorae represent wine, as oil, fruit and fish sauce were also imported in quantity. Nor, it would seem, did the imported wines appeal to all tastes. British beer offered strong competition and was important enough for its price to be fixed in the price edict issued in the late third century during the reign of Diocletian. This British beer certainly seems to have had its admirers since its price was fixed at twice that of Egyptian beer!

British duffel coat, the *birrus Britannicus,* and a special type of woollen rug, the *tapete Britannicum.* One of the fourth-century state weaving-mills providing army uniforms is known to have been in Britain. The mill operated in a town and, although its location is unknown, limited evidence including an excavated carding comb has led to Caerwent being suggested as a possible candidate.

A good indicator of trading systems is pottery as ceramic production was clearly an important commercial activity in Roman Britain and one which included both domestic and

A samian bowl. This bright red-glass pottery, imported from Gaul, was the most common high-status table-ware in Roman Britain.

imported wares. One of the sought-after imported wares was samian, a red-coated tableware imported from Gaul and Italy. Samian was often intricately decorated, with many examples having been made in moulds. Other examples were impressed with stamps or rouletted, and many were stamped with the maker's name. With its distinctive styles and maker's marks, samian can be closely dated and it is, therefore, a very useful archaeological tool which is found in considerable quantities at sites like Caerleon and Caerwent. Another ceramic type which is very common on these sites is the black-burnished native pottery produced by British potters such as those of the Durotriges of Dorset. The pots, often cooking pots, were durable, cheap and popular with the army. Military contracts were issued, and this native pottery found its way to virtually every Roman military site in Britain and dominated some assemblages at sites like Caerleon.

There was also significant local production. In the early years of the conquest, pottery was often associated with tile-manufacturing centres which produced items like the roof tiles, *tegulae* and *imbrices,* required by the army. There were two early production centres in Wales. A works depot at Holt, for example, functioned as a military tile factory supplying the fortress at Chester. At Usk there is even evidence suggesting that tile-makers or potters from the Rhineland and the Danube had been brought to Wales. With time, a number of small potteries were established at various places, leading to considerable variation in local ceramic traditions. A case in point is production in Caerleon where the fortress and large associated civil settlement would have created a very significant local market. Caerleon ware is found widely in and around the fortress as are examples of distinctive *mortaria* with smooth, red-coated exteriors and large quartz grits. One site of production for both was the kiln discovered on the golf-course site above Bulmore north of the fortress. The last firing in the kiln was still in place and included examples of both wares. There were eventually other important local kilns in places like Caldicot near Caerwent.

Coups and counter-coups

Economic sophistication, growing trade and *civitas* administration might suggest increasing stability in Romano-British society. It is important to remember, however, that the whole of the imperial system continued to depend on the army which remained at the forefront of affairs in Britain, a fact which had considerable significance for developments in Wales. When Hadrian ordered work to begin on his frontier wall in AD 122, for example, troops from all three legions in Britain were involved in its construction. Inscriptions confirm that a significant portion of the Second Augustan legion was assigned to the wall, leaving only a caretaker garrison at Caerleon. Predictably, repair and reconstruction work was necessary when the bulk of the legion returned to its permanent base. The legion was also engaged in construction of the Antonine Wall, a turf defence erected between the Forth and the Clyde in AD 142–4. Significant as these developments in imperial strategy undoubtedly were, it is also important to remember that during much of the long history of Roman Britain, many troop movements and associated political upheavals were the result of internal power struggles between contesting generals. Even in the early years of conquest, a civil war had placed Vespasian on the imperial throne. In subsequent years, a series of military coups were to shape the government of Rome, often with very direct implications for Wales and the rest of Britain.

An important example is presented by events in AD 192 when the emperor Commodus was assassinated and the Praetorian Guard effectively auctioned the throne to the highest bidder. Generals in the provinces, however, used their troops to advance their own claims to power. Notable among them were the North African Septimius Severus and Decimus Clodius Albinus, the governor of Britain. The ensuing power struggle reached its climax in AD 197 when Albinus withdrew most of the British legions and struck into Gaul, only to be defeated and killed in a bloody battle at Lyon. Among the troops known to have supported this ill-fated venture were men of the Second Augustan legion at Caerleon. Interestingly, in the aftermath the legion was replenished and restoration work at the fortress was commissioned by the victorious Severus. An inscription from Caerleon confirms these repairs and attributes the work to Severus and his sons, Caracalla and Geta. We can deduce that the work was completed before 211, the year in which Geta was murdered by his brother, because the Caerleon monument provides confirmation of the fratricide. Geta's name has been carefully excised from the inscription. Nor was this incident the end of political murder in Rome. The emperor Severus Alexander was assassinated in 235 and Gordian III was murdered in 244. During this period of political anarchy, troops from Britain were often among those involved in the power struggles on the Continent.

Soon other problems began to bedevil Rome as the imperial frontiers came under increasing pressure from external threats. Along the northern frontier of the empire, including Britain, danger was posed by seaborne Frankish, Irish and Saxon raiders. Their raids prompted a reorganization of Roman military forces and the building of what are usually described as the Saxon Shore forts. While threats from sea raiders were clearly real, this description may in a sense be misleading since there were also fears of internal threats in an increasingly less stable empire. For whatever reasons, there was a reorientation of troops in both north and south Wales. Northern coastal defences were concentrated at Caergybi and Caernarfon while, in the south, the old fort at Cardiff was rebuilt and eventually replaced Caerleon as the regional military centre. At Caerleon, occupation continued into the fourth century but this may have been a largely, and at times exclusively, civilian presence.

Some of these changes in the late third century were overseen by M. Mausaeus Carausius, the commander of the Classis Britannica, the Channel Fleet. Carausius seems to have enjoyed considerable success against barbarian raiders but there were accusations that these successes were based on prior knowledge of the raiders' movements. Carausius was accused of failing to act on his intelligence until after raids had been mounted and then of keeping the booty from their capture for himself. There may have been very good practical reasons to strike at heavily laden outwardly bound vessels, but the accusations were taken seriously enough by the emperor Maximian who ordered his commander in Britain to be executed. The response by Carausius was to follow the by then well-worn path of revolt; he seized Britain and declared himself emperor in AD 286 or 287. He was initially successful and for a time enjoyed the loyalty of troops in Gaul as well as Britain, allowing him to control both sides of the English Channel. When his influence in Gaul declined, however, Carausius was murdered by Allectus who has been described as his 'right-hand man'. Allectus proclaimed himself emperor in AD 293 and it was not until 296 that Constantius destroyed the rebel regime and restored imperial control in Britain.

Imperial control, however, continued to be eroded by both external and internal threats. It may well be the case that, as the fourth century unfolded, there was an increasing tendency for matters like defence to be approached on a regional or local level. A case in point seems to have been the Silurian *civitas* capital at Caerwent where there were significant modifications in the defences of the town. Particularly important were a series of semi-octagonal projecting towers which were built into the walls, probably between about AD 330 and 340. One of these towers survives in good repair today and joist-holes suggest that two wooden floors were built into the tower which would have had a wooden roof that could have provided a platform for a *ballista*. The towers were clearly not bonded into the wall and consequently should be interpreted as later additions. It is possible that the idea for the towers came from Cardiff where similar towers had recently been erected, bonded into the wall and became an integral part of the defences of the shore fort there. At about the same time that the towers were being built, the south gate at Caerwent was closed, being completely blocked by a well-made regularly coursed wall. With six towers extending from the south wall and the south gate sealed, Caerwent had dramatically improved defences on the side of the town facing what may increasingly have been perceived as a threatening sea. Interestingly, access through the north gate was also restricted, but clearly here some means of relatively easy communication was still required as a smaller gate was retained within the largely blocked arched entrance.

As these developments were unfolding in Wales, other parts of Roman Britain were also under threat. The Roman historian Ammianus Marcellinus described a 'barbarian conspiracy' – a co-ordinated attack in the north of England by Saxons, Franks, Scots and Picts in AD 367. In the following year, Count Theodosius was sent to restore military control. Soon, however, internal politics again led to a withdrawal of troops and these developments should probably be seen as the beginning, or perhaps more accurately, the acceleration of the end of Roman Britain. Central to these developments was the commander of the army, Magnus Maximus, Macsen Wledig in Welsh, who probably held the title *dux Britanniarum*, a British leader or duke.

Myth-making and Macsen

Welsh tradition says that Macsen married Elen, a princess from north Wales, and that he gave her three castles located at Caernarfon, Carmarthen and Caerleon. Maximus has traditionally been associated with Caernarfon and in one of the much later tales of the *Mabinogi*, *Breuddwyd Macsen* – the Dream of Macsen Wledig – he was already emperor. The throne, however, had been usurped and Macsen set out for Rome with Elen's brothers and the men of Segontium to regain it.

In AD 383, Maximus claimed the western empire and launched an attack on the emperor Gratian by striking into Gaul. We should remember that for almost a hundred years the empire had been effectively divided into two parts, east and west, each with a senior and a junior emperor, an Augustus and a Caesar. When Gratian was killed, Maximus was left in control of Britain, Gaul and Spain, becoming the senior Augustus in the west. In the short term, the situation seemed to have been accepted by Theodosius I, the eastern emperor, and it appeared that this military intervention from Britain would succeed. In 388, however, Theodosius mounted a lightning strike and in the ensuing conflict, Maximus was killed.

When Maximus led his armies into Gaul, he removed most, if not all, of the front-line Roman troops in Britain. It is doubtful that they were ever replaced as permanent contingents in such strength again. Moreover, Maximus seems to have implemented contingency plans for local defence before departing and, in doing

A coin of Magnus Maximus, Macsen Wledig in Welsh tradition.

so, may have accelerated the sorts of changes that were already occurring in places like Caerwent. There seems to have been deliberate devolution of responsibility for local defence and, where possible, this responsibility would have passed to the urban-based tribal leaderships already in place in the *civitates*. Where this was not possible, it would have been necessary to employ other strategies. It is possible that Cunedda, by tradition a leader of the Votadini from the area of the Firth of Forth in Scotland, came to north Wales at this time. Later tales credit Cunedda with expelling the Irish from Gwynedd and it is interesting that when the Welsh kingdoms of the fifth century emerged, some claimed descent from Maximus, Cunedda or both, presumably in an attempt to establish an air of legitimacy for the ruling dynasty. It is true that the defeat of Maximus does not quite mark the end of Roman military activity in Britain. Between AD 396 and 398, for example, the Vandal general Stilicho brought troops to Britain and campaigned in the north. By 401, however, pressures on Italy itself led to the recall of Stilicho and his forces. In 409, during another period of military anarchy, which was in part a consequence of yet another bid for power launched from Britain, British authorities renounced allegiance to the usurping Constantine III. Interestingly, the historian Zosimus, writing at the beginning of the sixth century, tells us that during this period Britain revolted and rejected Roman authority altogether. He says that the circumstances associated with the barbarian advances 'brought the people of Britain and some of the Gaulish nations to the point that they revolted from Roman rule and lived by themselves, no longer obeying Roman laws'. Zosimus continues, 'the Britons took arms and fighting for themselves freed their cities from the barbarian pressure' and suggests that in doing so they provided a role model for the Amoricans and other Gaulish tribes who attempted to follow their example. Perhaps not surprisingly, in AD 410 the emperor Honorius issued his 'rescript' in which Rome renounced responsibility for Britain and instructed local authorities to look after their own affairs. It seems clear that in parts of Wales, as in other parts of Britain, many had already been doing so for some time.

The rise of Christianity

One of the key elements in later Roman Britain was the rise of Christianity, a religion with an increasingly widespread appeal based on its unique combination of monotheism, high ethical principles and a promise of salvation. The initial Roman response to Christianity was one of hostility to what was perceived as a secretive society which rejected the imperial cult. A consequence of this perception was a series of persecutions leading to widespread martyrdom and it is known that some of these persecutions spread into Britain. Three early Christian martyrs in Britain, Alban, Julius and Aaron, are known by name. Significantly, two of the three, Julius and Aaron, died in Wales. Both were executed, almost certainly at the same time, in Caerleon. While it is impossible to say with confidence exactly when the deaths took place, it seems likely to have been during one of a series of persecutions that occurred in the mid-third century. Beyond this incident, which confirms an early Christian presence in Wales, there is little direct historical or archaeological evidence for Christian practice during the third century. It may be, however, that changes in funerary practice, notably the shift from cremation to inhumation which was seen in places like Caerleon, were prompted in part by an increasing Christian influence.

What is well documented is the dramatic change in fortune for Christianity which occurred after Constantine's notable victory in the battle at the Milvian Bridge in AD 312. Constantine, soon to become 'Constantine the Great', attributed his victory over his rival Maxentius to the intervention of the Christian God whose symbol of the cross he had adopted for the battle. The almost immediate consequence was the 'Peace of the Church' in 313, which made Christianity legal in the empire. Soon the influence of the Church became even greater as Constantine transferred powers previously vested exclusively in the magistrates to the Christian bishops. In legal actions, for example, either party could demand that a case be transferred from the courts to the local bishop for adjudication. Significantly, within two years of the Peace of the Church, a Council was held at Arles which was attended by three British bishops and by representatives of a fourth. This representation confirms that an episcopal structure was in place and, as will be seen, it is perfectly reasonable to assume that one of these bishoprics was in Wales.

Some of the most persuasive evidence for Christian worship in fourth-century Wales comes from Caerwent, the *civitas* capital of the Silures. Excavation of a house near the centre of the town, for example, revealed an urn which had been buried to floor level. Covered by an inverted bowl, the urn contained a number of pots, a flanged pewter bowl, a pewter plate, a knife and a double swivel-hook as well as fragments of woollen cloth. On the base of the bowl was a *chi-rho* symbol, one of the most widely employed early Christian symbols. The two letters begin the Greek word *Christos* or Christ. The Greek capital *chi* is written as a capital X and *rho* (the Greek 'r') as a capital P, usually superimposed so that it intersected the X. The symbol was frequently circled and eventu-ally evolved into a wheeled cross. Its presence at Caerwent is compelling evidence for Christianity in the town and it has even been suggested that the assemblage recovered from the urn represents utensils to be used in the early Christian tradition of *agape* (a supper of 'friendly affection' frequently held in private homes after the Eucharist).

Interestingly, the idea of domestic worship may impact on other finds from Caerwent. One of the archaeological problems associ-ated with early Christianity is the difficulty in identifying a church or other site of worship. One of the main reasons for this difficulty is that, well into the fourth century, Christian groups tended to meet in houses and it can be difficult to interpret these house churches as other than domestic sites. There is, however, one house in Caerwent which may have had a demonstrable ecclesi-astical role. Located in the north-east corner of the town is a house

The resurgence of paganism

While Christianity was clearly well established with an episcopal structure in place in fourth-century Britain, and the religion had adherents in places like the Silurian *civitas* capital, it is impossible to say with confidence how widespread Christian belief may have been. It is also difficult to know whether Christianity was more common among certain classes of society. Whatever the case, there were certainly still challenges from within as well as from outside the early Christian community. Pagan belief, for example, remained strong and Julian, emperor AD 360–63, actively encouraged pagan cults in an attempt to re-establish traditional Roman religious practice. Several late pagan temples were built as a part of the process. One of the best-known examples is the temple complex at Lydney overlooking the Severn which was dedicated to the healing-god Nodens. It is worth remembering too that the re-excavated temple complex near the forum in Caerwent was late, probably built sometime after AD 330. Moreover, there is evidence that the temple was refurbished some three or four decades later, perhaps during the reign of Julian, the 'Apostate'.

which was excavated in 1909. The structure seems to have been altered substantially in the fourth century when, among other modifications, an apse was built onto a room in one wing of the building creating a relatively large hall (approximately 7m by 4m). The main floor surface was of plain red mosaic, with a coloured mosaic surface in the apse. The hall was flanked by a range of smaller rooms and George Boon, formerly Keeper of Archaeology in the National Museum of Wales, suggested that the whole range of rooms could have been used for Christian worship. Particularly interesting in this context is one of the smaller flanking rooms with a rough stone floor, or perhaps more accurately stone floor foundation which, on the basis of comparison with other sites, Boon thought to have been a baptistery. Examples of shallow circular tanks made of lead have been found in similar locations on other sites, sometimes with *chi-rho* symbols, suggesting that the tanks were used for baptism. If this interpretation is correct, it is important because during this period the sacrament of baptism was administered by a bishop. The implication is that, at least at times, a bishop was resident in Caerwent and it is not unreasonable to assume that one of the bishops represented at Arles had a base in Wales. There is another important conclusion to be drawn from the evidence for early Christian worship at Caerwent. A clue is presented in the life of saint Tatheus or Tathan, who established a monastery at Caerwent. This life describes how the founder was invited to the town to provide *evangelica hortamenta,* evangelical exhortation, not conversion. If, as a consequence, we assume that Tatheus came to an already Christian community, a strong case can be made for uninterrupted Christian worship in Caerwent from the late Roman period to the present day.

Challenges to 'conventional' Christian worship also came from within the Church itself. One of the most important challenges to accepted orthodoxy was Pelagianism which had its roots in Britain. Pelagius was a theologian born in Britain sometime in the second half of the fourth century. There is a tradition that places his birth in Wales, possibly at Usk, although there is no firm evidence to support that view. What is more certain is that he studied law in Rome in the 380s and that in 386 he entered the Church. Contemporary accounts suggest that he was a man of formidable stature, a 'monstrous great Goliath' in the words of Paulus Orosius. Clearly less than favourably disposed to Pelagius, Orosius was an active supporter of St Augustine of Hippo. At this time, Augustine was busily writing about the human relationship with God and in doing so defining conventional orthodoxy. That orthodoxy suggested that all people were totally subject to Divine Will and that only Divine Grace could bring salvation. Pelagius rejected this predeterminism and argued instead for free will and individual responsibility for salvation. It was for individuals to decide whether to act rightly or wrongly in the Pelagian view. Carried to its logical conclusion, this philosophy brought into question ideas such as original sin. How could God, who forgives people their own sins, hold them responsible for those of someone else? Pelagius argued his case in Rome from about 394 until the sack of Rome by Alaric in 410. After that date, he fled to North Africa and eventually to the Holy Land. While his teachings were branded as heretical he gained many adherents in the Mediterranean; interestingly, he also seems to have had a strong following in Britain.

It may have been that a visit to Britain by Victricius, the bishop of Rouen, probably in 403, was to counter the growth of the

Pelagian heresy in Britain. That was certainly the reason that St Germanus of Auxerre, accompanied by Lupus, the bishop of Troyes, came to Britain in 429. According to Constantius, a monk in Lyon who wrote the life of Germanus, a delegation sent from Britain to bishops in Gaul sought help in overcoming the Pelagian heresy which was said to be increasingly dominating British Christianity. In the story written by Constantius, preaching circuits, a public meeting and the working of a miracle allowed Germanus to triumph. Caution should always be employed in taking such accounts too literally but there are interesting descriptive passages which may tell us a great deal about Britain in the immediate post-Roman period. The Pelagian faction, for example, is described as being led by members of the nobility accompanied by large numbers of their retainers. Conspicuous riches and brilliant dress are descriptions applied to the Pelagians. A number of important points are implied in this account. In the first place, it seems clear that significant numbers of the British aristocracy had embraced Pelagianism, and it has been suggested that a doctrine placing emphasis on free will and self-reliance may have had a particular appeal to people actively attempting to sever their long-standing links with Rome. Moreover, a display of wealth including high-quality multi-coloured clothing reminds us that nearly two decades after the rescript of Honorius, a confident and prosperous aristocracy remained in place in Britain. There is no reason to think that in parts of Wales there was any less confidence and prosperity than was found in the south-east of what had been the province, or indeed that there was any less attachment to the doctrines of Pelagius. Perhaps the most important conclusion to be drawn, however, is that the reaction to the perceived threat of heresy can be seen as confirming the importance of Christianity in the immediate post-Roman period and it is no surprise that Christianity became one of the decisive elements in shaping early medieval society.

The end of Roman Britain

The end of Roman Britain was a process and not an event. As has been seen, in later Roman Britain there was considerable prosperity with a well-developed villa economy and sophisticated industrial systems. Roman Wales, while undoubtedly retaining unique and distinctive aspects of its tribal past, was also a part of a Continental system linked by trade, industry and common governmental processes. The situation was, however, far from stable as the Roman system was increasingly threatened and ultimately undermined in part by external forces. Arguably as significant, however, was continuing and accelerating internal unrest. Britain, including Wales, at times played a key role in a succession of political upheavals as coups and counter-coups racked the empire. At other times, the insularity of Britain must have seemed a welcome buffer to Continental intrigue. Eventually, the bond with Rome was formally broken, but trade links and other forms of interaction were not. Significantly, as the description of the visit by Germanus confirms, prosperity did not evaporate with the formal end of political links with Rome.

One of the most important developments in the fourth century empire was the rise of Christianity, and there is good evidence of early Christian practice and continuing Christian influences in Wales. Places like Caerwent, the *civitas* capital of the Silures, became early centres of Christian worship. The pagan revival and the Pelagian heresy may have threatened conventional Christianity, but on the eve of the birth of the early medieval period there can be no doubt that Christianity was a very important element in shaping the emergence of new social and political systems. As these systems developed, Wales itself also emerged as a recognizable entity.

5 The Early Medieval Period

Political readjustments

The pattern of political development in early to mid-fifth-century Britain is far from clear. There are, however, references to Vortigern (Gwrtheyrn in Welsh tradition), an early high king who seems to have had interests in Kent as well as in Powys. An important piece of evidence relating to Vortigern is the long inscription found on the ninth-century pillar of Eliseg which names Gwrtheyrn as the founder of the kingdom of Powys as well as claiming for the ruling dynasty descent from Magnus Maximus himself. The sixth-century monk Gildas, who is often our only written source for this period, described Vortigern as *superbus tyrannus* (proud ruler) and recounted the now well-known story of how he gave land to the Saxons in return for military service. There is probably an element of truth in the story; if Gildas was right in suggesting that Vortigern faced a threat from the Picts and the Scots while also fearing an attack from Rome, it may have seemed sensible to him to employ Saxons as *foederati*. There were certainly precedents for recruiting German mercenaries and allowing them to settle on land in return for military service, and the suggestion that such a Saxon settlement was established in Kent is consistent with the archaeological evidence there. There is also evidence that these imported troops revolted sometime before 450 and in doing so gained control over other parts of south-eastern England. While this was happening, it seems that rival factions were emerging within Romano-British society. Vortigern, for example, was said to have been opposed by Ambrosius Aurelianus, whose family is described by Gildas as having 'worn the purple', that is to have been of senatorial or imperial standing.

A number of different models have been suggested to explain this apparent regional variation. An attractive one is that the retention of tribal identity was very much stronger in the west. It can be argued that in the highly romanized province created in the south-east of England, the pre-conquest tribal systems declined rapidly. As an unarmed peasantry was considered essential to a well-ordered Roman society the élite, in keeping with Roman practice, would have relied on the army, which increasingly meant mercenary troops

Britons and Saxons

The traditional explanation to describe this period suggests that Saxons as well as Angles and Jutes continued to arrive in increasing numbers, leading to protracted conflict and the inexorable advance to the west of the newcomers. Surviving Romano-British communities perished or were, in this simplified model, forced to flee west as refugees. A growing body of evidence, however, suggests that the model is flawed. There is, for example, little if any basis for believing that a large-scale exodus occurred from the south-east. What seems more likely is that the existing communities there simply reached an accommodation with new overlords and that, in time, they accepted the language, religion and political/social systems of the new élite through a process of acculturation. What is particularly important in terms of Welsh history, however, is that it also seems clear that there was a fundamentally different reaction to these changing circumstances in the west of Britain, particularly in Wales.

such as the *foederati,* to maintain order. When that system began to unravel with the Saxon settlement, a peasantry seeing itself as deriving little benefit from the old order may have been happy enough to reach an accommodation with a new one. In areas like Wales, where resistance to the Roman advance had been protracted and bitter and where in many areas *civitas* administration was never put in place, however, the situation was different. As will be seen, even in south-east Wales, where the *civitas* was well established and presumably effective, there is good reason to believe that there was considerable survival of tribal identity and tradition. This being the case, it comes as no surprise that different strategies for self-defence were adopted and that resistance to Saxon military advances remained strong. More archaeological evidence is required to allow us to test such assumptions more fully but this interpretation seems to provide a good working model to give us a context for explaining developments in the fifth century and later.

The emergence of the kingdoms

The political systems which emerged in early post-Roman Wales evolved within regional kingdoms. Sometimes these political entities could be quite small; Ergyng, a Welsh kingdom north-east of modern Monmouth in what is today Herefordshire is a case in point. It is worth remembering too that there was sometimes fractionalization of larger kingdoms with, for example, Gwent Iscoed, the south-eastern corner of Gwent, at times being controlled by a separate dynasty from the rest of the region. What is particularly interesting, however, is the location of the larger kingdoms which emerged. The key point to note is the apparently close relationship between the early medieval kingdoms and the assumed tribal territories of the pre-conquest Iron Age. The kingdom of Powys, for example, appears to have emerged from the *civitas* of the Cornovii although it is likely that the political centre of the kingdom shifted from the *civitas* capital at Wroxeter to the hillfort of the Wrekin. The interpretation of the name of the kingdom raises some questions but it is generally thought to derive from the Latin *pagenses,* which can be translated as 'people of the countryside'. As has been seen, the ruling dynasty in Powys claimed descent not only from Gwrtheyrn but also from Magnus Maximus. Given its assumed origins in the *civitas* and claims of association with the ill-fated emperor, it might be expected that Powys would demonstrate strong survivals of *romanitas.* Nevertheless, we have good indications of very strong Iron Age influences. The irascible monk Gildas, who may have been educated at Illtud's monastery in Llantwit Major (Welsh Llanilltud Fawr), decried the state of Britain in his *De Excidio Britanniae* (The Ruin of Britain), and attacked the kings of his time. One of his targets was the king of Powys and his account seems to transport us directly back to the Iron Age. The king was named Cuneglasus, the most 'British' name to be found in the text of Gildas. Moreover, it is perfectly possible to interpret that text as describing Cuneglasus as driving a chariot and living in a hillfort!

The situation in Dyfed is also interesting and in some respects similar. As will be seen, there was a strong Irish influence in southwest Wales as well as in Brycheiniog which seems to have been closely associated. At times, Ceredigion also seems to have been closely linked, but this kingdom's affiliation oscillated between Dyfed and Gwynedd. Whatever the nature of these linkages, there is a demonstrable development of the kingdom of Dyfed from the

The Vortipor memorial. This bilingual inscription is written in Latin script and ogam.

civitas of the Demetae where there are good indications that, despite an accommodation with Irish settlers and the long Roman occupation, the old tribal identity survived. In some respects the small *civitas* capital at Carmarthen may have been atypical and, in comparison with most *civitates*, less than fully romanized. This uneven imposition of *romanitas*, in its turn, may have been an important contributory factor in the native survival.

In the south-east, the kingdoms of Gwent and Glywysing emerged, eventually giving rise to Glamorgan (Morgannwg). It is reasonable to assume that, as with Powys, the origins of kingship in Gwent are to be sought in the *civitas*. Indeed, the name Gwent itself is derived directly from Venta, the Roman name for the *civitas* capital which by this time must have been described as Caer, the fortress, of Venta. Again, we would expect a significant residue of *romanitas* in this area, given the focus of the *civitas*, a number of known villa sites and a late Roman military presence, at least in Cardiff. There is, however, an impressive body of evidence suggesting strong survival of native influences in the land of the Silures. This is the case even within Caerwent itself. For example, the carved sandstone head found on a platform, in what is apparently a shrine associated with a house, in one of the western *insulae* is purely native in its inspiration. It and other objects from the town such as a seated mother-goddess indicate the survival of native cult practices, and it is significant that the contexts of these finds suggest that they were in place at the height of the Roman town. Other small finds appear to confirm such long-standing native influences and, consequently, it is prudent to think that there was considerable cultural diversity with both native and Roman traditions mixing in Caerwent. Certainly, inscriptions confirm the survival of the tribal name, particularly the early third-century 'Paulinus' stone which acknowledges the *respublica civitatis Silurum*. If native influence and tribal identity survived in the *civitas* capital, and the evidence strongly suggests that they did, then we would assume that such survival would be even stronger in the countryside. In this respect, the Thornwell Farm site is particularly interesting. If we accept circularity in house-design as native, the very late roundhouses at Thornwell tell us that native lifestyles survived well into the fourth century almost in the shadow of the *civitas* capital. Assuming that this was the case, the Silurian highland may have had only the thinnest veneer of *romanitas*. A previously discussed written source contributes to this discussion: as has been seen, there is evidence of early Christianity in Caerwent and an account of the establishment of a monastery there by Tatheus who was invited to provide *evangelica hortamenta* to the residents there. The existence of the monastery seems to be confirmed archaeologically by two early

Christian cemeteries at Caerwent, one located around the church and the other being an extramural burial ground outside the East Gate; radiocarbon dating places the burials between the fifth and tenth centuries. We are told that Tatheus was attracted to Caerwent to establish his monastery by the promise of a grant of land there. The promise came from the king of Gwent, Caradog. It is interesting and important that the name Caradog, Caratacus, with its strong associations with the resistance to Rome, should be remembered in Silurian territory and that it should be deemed appropriate for an early medieval king. The obvious conclusion to be drawn is that some aspects of native tradition must have remained very strong indeed among the Silures.

By the sixth century, the most powerful of the Welsh kingdoms was Gwynedd. Gildas was particularly scathing in his attack on Maglocunus (Maelgwn), the king of Gwynedd, but he acknowledged his power. One of several less than flattering descriptions he used for the king was 'mightier than many in both power and malice'. It may be the case that Maelgwn seized power on the mainland from a base in what was originally a sub-kingdom on Anglesey and that the name Gwynedd commemorates his tribe or sub-tribe which lived on the island. The name Ordovices, however, survived in Merioneth where there was a *cantref* Orddwy, the hundred of the Ordovices. The early history of Gwynedd is complicated by the Cunedda story and the suggestion that the Votadini were instrumental in its foundation. The evidence here is very limited although excavation of square-ditched barrows at Tandderwen may indicate some form of contact with Scotland. It is, of course, possible that the origins of the kingdom can be found in late Roman tradition given the continuing role of sites like Segontium. It seems more likely, however, that in what must have been one of the least romanized parts of Wales, the old tribal aristocracy survived and reasserted itself in the post-Roman period. Whatever the case, by the sixth and seventh centuries Gwynedd was generally recognized as the strongest military power among the Welsh kingdoms.

Early medieval type-sites

Given the limitations of available historical evidence, we must rely heavily on archaeology to assist us in understanding early medieval political and social development in Wales. A number of indicators may be particularly helpful; for example, high-status reoccupation of hillfort sites may provide good evidence for an assertion of kingship or, at the very least, aristocratic control in an area. There are excavated sites in Gwynedd which may be placed in this category; Dinas Emrys, above the Glaslyn Valley, is a particularly good example. There has been a long-standing temptation to equate Emrys with the Ambrosius named by Gildas and to place his confrontation with Vortigern, which is described in the ninth-century *Historia Brittonum*, at the site, although there is no real archaeological basis for doing so. There is, however, good evidence of late Roman occupation including distinctive late third- or fourth-century *mortaria* and other pottery forms from that period. There are also fragments of glass from the site which are probably late Roman in date. In addition to this material, there are also more than forty fragments of an amphora dating from the fifth or sixth century and a sherd cut into a disc shape

Degannwy Castle in Gwynedd is one of several Iron Age sites with evidence of early medieval reoccupation.

with a *chi-rho* symbol which is probably also early medieval. This evidence allows us to say with confidence that Dinas Emrys demonstrates élite-site continuity into the early medieval period. The same may be true of Degannwy Castle; late Roman occupation here can be clearly demonstrated with a range of artefacts dating from the second to the late fourth century. Also found on the site was an amphora sherd giving a late fifth- or early sixth-century date and a fragment of glass probably dating from about the same time. There are later references, particularly the *Annales Cambriae,* which claim an association of the site with Maelgwn. What we can safely say on the basis of the archaeological evidence available to us is that Degannwy is another example of élite-site continuity. A third site in the north, which may fall into this category, is Dinorben although the evidence for early medieval activity here is less clear.

Coygan Camp

Indications that some hilltop sites were favoured for high-status occupation in the early medieval period are also found in the south. A case in point was Coygan Camp, once a promontory fort overlooking Carmarthen Bay but now destroyed by quarrying. Excavations conducted in the 1960s confirmed that the site was occupied in the Iron Age and Roman periods. In addition, an amphora sherd and fragments of distinctive red slipware pottery point not only to an early medieval date but also to trade, either directly or indirectly, with the Mediterranean at that time. Again, the clear indication of these findings is that there was high-status occupation of the site in the sixth century.

Similar high-status occupation can be demonstrated at what is probably the best-known early medieval site in Wales, Dinas Powys. Today Dinas Powys is a village about four miles south-west of Cardiff; the top of a limestone ridge there was investigated by Leslie Alcock who excavated the site between 1954 and 1958. The excavation confirmed multiphase occupation and while there has been considerable discussion about dating sequences and a rephasing of some of the features it is obvious that the main occupation was early medieval. Stone-revetted banks and ditches cut off the neck of the promontory and, within the enclosure formed by these features, drip gullies defined two sub-rectangular buildings which are generally interpreted as a hall and a barn. There were also three well-constructed stone-lined hearths and a number of small bowl hearths. The most striking aspect of the site is the range of finds associated with it. There were more than eighty sherds of fine red slipwares and no fewer than 170 sherds of amphorae which probably originated in North Africa or the eastern Mediterranean. Also found were fragments of grey bowls which were probably made in the Bordeaux region of France and other Continental wares including coarse beige-coloured jars which are likely to have originated in north-west France. Some of the slipwares had stamped animal designs which Alcock interpreted as 'running felines'.

In addition to the ceramic finds there was also a significant quantity of glass fragments representing some forty glass vessels, mainly cone-shaped beakers and bowls which were almost certainly Continental, and probably Anglo-Saxon in origin. There was evidence of iron-working on site including ore, slag and furnace-linings. Bronze-casting also took place on site as lidded crucibles were recovered in the excavations; these contained bronze and gold residues. These crucibles probably relate to a fragmentary lead die for making zoomorphic penannular brooches that was also found. The design of the brooch suggests Irish influences and may even indicate that a jeweller was working on the site. There is good evidence for other types of craft production as well. Spindle-whorls, a loom weight and a bobbin show that spinning and weaving also took place at Dinas Powys. There were double-sided bone combs, probably meant to be worn in the hair, and a bone gaming-piece. Rotary querns confirm an ability to grind corn and suggest that there was arable production in the surrounding area to supply the site. Animal-bones, dominated by pig, suggest that the inhabitants enjoyed a rich diet. This impressively large and varied artefact assemblage gives a date range of late fifth to seventh century and leaves us in no doubt that Dinas Powys was an important high-status site of the early medieval period. The evidence for trade contact with the Mediterranean and northern Europe is impressive as are the indications of a range of industrial activities on site. All the evidence suggests a prosperous defended settlement enjoying active contact, either directly or indirectly, with Europe and beyond. The best interpretation for all of this material would seem to be that Dinas Powys was a *llys*, or proto-*llys*, the court of a

Welsh lord and there are interesting parallels with later excavated *llysoedd* sites.

Llys and llan

If we are correct in interpreting Dinas Powys as the site of a *llys*, it is a very early example of what became a central unit of administration in later medieval Wales. The later Welsh law tracts provide us with a model for land use and administration. An important fiscal unit was the *maenor, maenol* in north Wales, which was generally made up of four *trefi* which today would be translated as towns but which, in this context, would be better understood as agricultural estates. Twelve *maenorau* plus two *trefi* made up a *cwmwd* (commote) and two commotes formed a *cantref* (hundred). The two extra *trefi* in each commote were reserved for the king who also received other renders from each *maenor.* There would usually have been upland and lowland holdings associated with the units, providing summer and winter pasture. The concept of multiple estates implied by this structure provided the basis for the later medieval Welsh agrarian system, and it may have been the case that this system was in place generally in Wales from the early medieval period. In this system each *maenor* would have required a central administrative centre, a *llys.* Moreover, given the strong Christian influences in the region, each would also have required a religious focus, a *llan.* The term *llan* is usually translated as church today but it originally referred to the enclosure, generally a circular enclosure, around the church. If Dinas Powys is an early example of a *llys,* recent excavation suggests that archaeologists working nearby may have discovered the site of an associated *llan.*

Approximately one mile from Dinas Powys is Llandough, where there is a church dedicated to St Dochdwy who probably lived in the fifth century. A cross-shaft survives in the churchyard, which stylistically would be dated to the late tenth or early eleventh century. The Llandaf Charters refer to a monastery on the site in the eighth century and the foundation could, of course, be even earlier. There is also the site of a Roman villa which was excavated in 1977–8 to the south of the church. In 1990, planning permission was given for a housing estate and funding from the developer provided for a small excavation near the churchyard which was undertaken by the Cotswold Archaeological Trust. This assessment confirmed that the area was a cemetery site, and the developers agreed to fund a complete excavation. The results have been remarkable. A total of 858 burials were recovered as well as 152 groups of disarticulated bones. Of the burials, more than 400 were in a good state of preservation with evidence of wooden coffins in sixteen cases and stone-lined burials in another fourteen.

The excavated cemetery site consists of four areas. Area One was nearest the churchyard and seems to have begun as a late Roman cemetery. One Roman coin was recovered and there were five 'hob-nail boot burials' which are diagnostic of Roman inhumations. It may be that when the villa was abandoned in the early fourth century, activity shifted up the hillside where, by the fifth century, a monastery had been established. A curved arc confined Area One in what was probably the original boundary of a curvilinear churchyard. Radiocarbon dates of AD 535 and 880 were obtained from burials in this area. Area Two, which was to the west, contained a burial in a wooden coffin which produced a date of 840. The curvilinear pattern emerged again in Area Three which was to the north and which contained a skeleton dated to 990. Area Four had the greatest concentration of burials on the site, with many children's graves and a number of examples of graves cutting one another. A response to a disaster such as plague could have produced this sort of pattern of inhumation. As there was a generally east–west orientation for the graves and few grave-goods, the assumption is that the site consisted of Christian burials. The artefactual evidence associated is sparse and much of the material such as Roman and Iron Age sherds was probably residual. Nevertheless, there are some very interesting objects including five sherds of amphorae from a type of vessel thought to have been used as an olive-oil container and shipped from Asia Minor. There are direct parallels with sherds found at nearby Dinas Powys. Some of the burials also contained distinctive white quartz pebbles similar to those which have been found on other early Christian sites in Wales. It is thought that a passage in Revelations, 'to him that overcometh will I give to eat of the hidden manna and will give him a white stone', provides the basis for this burial practice.

The idea of viewing Dinas Powys/Llandough as an example of *llys* and *llan* is an attractive one which reminds us of the close relationship between political and ecclesiastical authority in early medieval Wales. It is possible that Llandough would have been a *clas* church, a hereditary property-holding religious community. Certainly some monastic communities, particularly in the Vale of Glamorgan, became large and powerful while, in some cases, developing very widespread reputations as centres of learning. Llantwit Major (Llanilltud Fawr) and Llancarfan are good examples.

Monuments in stone

It would be helpful to have more excavated sites, both secular and ecclesiastic, to inform our understanding of this period. It is, however, frequently difficult to identify the sites and, in the case of religious foundations, often virtually impossible to excavate even when the sites are found. It is almost certainly the case that the sites of many early medieval churches lie under the post-conquest parish churches of today. Nevertheless, although early church sites are frequently inaccessible to us, in Wales we are fortunate to have other good types of religious evidence in the archaeological record. Particularly important are a number of inscriptions on stones. Most of these inscriptions are on funerary monuments and fifth-century examples frequently have the Latin formula *HIC IACET* (here lies). These memorial stones are very useful in providing further evidence of Christian influences and complement texts including the lives of saints such as Cadog, Dewi (David), Illtud, and Samson and other tracts associated with figures like Gildas and Patrick. As has been seen, inscribed stones also provide us with the names of kings and their claimed lines of descent. The Vortipor inscription on a stone found in the churchyard of Castell-dwyran in Dyfed, for example, provides excellent corroboration of Gildas and the long inscription on the pillar of Eliseg gives us a body of evidence relating to the emergence of Powys. Other royal names are provided by monumental inscriptions. A good example is Hywel ap Rhys, a ninth-century king of Glywysing, who erected an imposing memorial to his father at Llantwit Major.

The symbols on the stones are interesting, particularly the use of the *chi-rho* symbol which, in the fifth and sixth centuries, developed into a monogrammatic cross, that is one in which letters were overlaid or interwoven. There are good examples on stones from Penmachno and Treflys in Gwynedd. Interestingly, the

Maen Achwyfan, the stone of lamentations, near Whitford in Clwyd is an excellent example of a disc-headed cross-slab.

accompanying inscription on the Penmachno stone commemorates a fifth- or sixth-century figure named Carausius. The process of stylistic development continued, giving rise to the ring cross, frequently described as a Celtic cross, which was increasingly adopted from the seventh century onwards. By the tenth and eleventh centuries the result was the large and impressive high crosses such as those at Carew and Nevern in Dyfed and the *Maen Achwyfan* near Whitford in Clwyd which, with their intricate knotwork decoration, are among the most imposing standing monuments in Wales.

Classifying early Christian monuments

These early Christian monuments clearly provide a number of insights into early medieval Wales and consequently represent an important area for study. A scholar who made a particular contribution to this study was Victor Nash-Williams, Keeper of Archaeology, in the National Museum. In 1950, he published his classification system which still underpins current research. Nash-Williams divided the stones into three main early medieval categories. Group I consisted of inscribed stones dating from the fifth to the seventh century. Group II stones were cross-marked and dated from the seventh to the ninth century. Group III was made up of the cross slabs and high crosses of the ninth to the thirteenth century. A Group IV contained transitional Romanesque monuments dating from the eleventh to the thirteenth century. The system has required refinement, particularly since there are cross-marked stones earlier than the seventh century just as there are inscribed stones which are later. The Royal Commission devised a classification system with seven categories in an effort to address such problems. Nevertheless, the work of Nash-Williams has been very important in shaping the investigation of this important body of evidence.

As has already been noted, an interesting aspect of some of the inscriptions is the use of ogam. Ogam is an alphabetic script which seems to have been devised to write Irish. It consisted of four categories or sets of five letters or sounds which were expressed by lines or grooves running at different angles from a vertical base line giving a twenty-letter alphabet. In many cases, such as the Vortipor example, inscriptions are bilingual with the ogam text accompanying a Latin one. The implication of these inscriptions, which tend to be concentrated in Dyfed and Brycheiniog, is that there were significant Irish influences in the south-west. This may relate to a movement of the Deisi tribe from Leinster in south-east Ireland to Wales, a movement which may have occurred as early as the fourth century. It is possible that the Irish came as *foederati* settling in the *civitas* of the Demetae. Whatever the case, there seems to have been an accommodation between the Irish and the native population different from the apparently hostile confrontation in Gwynedd. Moreover, links with Ireland seem to have been maintained as is indicated by the important crannog site at Llangorse. A crannog is an artificial island and the example near the northern shore of Llangorse lake, unique in Wales, consisted of a built-up platform made of stone and timber. The plan and construction of the site have close parallels with sites in Ireland where there were a number of contemporary crannogs. When Llangorse was investigated archaeologically, the artefactual evidence recovered argued strongly for interpretation of the site as a *llys* of the king of Brycheiniog. It also seems likely, given the evidence relating to the destruction of the site, that the crannog was the target of an attack in AD 916 which is described in the Anglo-Saxon Chronicle.

The use of ogam and other indicators of Irish influence are interesting and clearly have language implications; there are other important linguistic indicators found on inscribed stones. One interesting suggestion is that the inscriptions themselves seem to have been increasingly influenced by manuscript forms. By the end of the sixth century, for example, half-uncial letter-forms based on 'bookhand' script were replacing the earlier rounded Roman capitals. The important early seventh-century Cadfan inscription, a memorial to a king of Gwynedd which is now at the church of Llangadwaladr, shows a mixture of the two styles. What is even more interesting is that it has been suggested that the form of the Latin name used in the inscription can be taken as evidence of the use of the Welsh language. Certainly, the appearance of Welsh names in the *Historia Brittonum* implies widespread use of the language and a case has been made that the eighth-century Towyn stone in Gwynedd represents the first known inscription in Welsh.

Early medieval Wales

The picture which emerges from this brief overview of Wales in the early medieval period is one of developing kingship, strong Christian influences and a considerable measure of social continuity. It is important for us to remember that there is good evidence for social sophistication during this period. Craft and industry, for example, did not end with the Romans. Artefacts such as distinctive penannular brooches were produced by skilled bronzesmiths. Interestingly, surviving fifth-century examples of these brooches seem to draw their inspiration from the Iron Age, reflecting tastes which may have continued throughout the Romano-British period. Finds of glass rods from sites such as Dinas Powys suggest the production of *millefiori* enamel. Finely made bone and antler combs remind us that personal appearance continued to be important. Dinas Powys also confirms the continuing significance of iron production and some of the iron tools recovered from the site remind us that leather and woodworking were important elements in the craft production 'portfolio'. It is very important to keep in mind the fact that organic remains including leather, wood and textiles only survive in unusual anaerobic conditions. As a consequence, much material from the early medieval period does not survive in the archaeological record. Occasional finds such as an intricately patterned cloth from the water-logged conditions at Llangorse, however, confirm the quality of the textiles produced. Containers of wood, leather and basketry would have continued to serve a community which, while largely aceramic, remained efficient and productive.

As has been seen, the Church was highly influential in shaping early medieval society, and notable monastic foundations earned reputations as centres of education and literacy. Trade links with the Continent and beyond were maintained and there were thriving craft industries on some élite sites. For all these reasons it is wholly inappropriate to describe this period, particularly in Wales and the west, as the Dark Ages. It was a period of transition and redefinition but not one of free-fall descent into cultural decay. Moreover, it was a period in which the Welsh language emerged and matured, providing a common element for the political entities which developed in western post-Roman Britain. The emergence of Wales was of the utmost historical importance, and the common cultural bonds which linked the emerging Welsh kingdoms bring us full circle to the 'Celtic debate' with which we began. It is obvious that elements of *romanitas* were transmitted from the late Roman to the early medieval period. Similarly, however, elements of native tradition with clear Iron Age antecedents also remained strong. Just as we require a term to describe the common cultural affinities of European Iron Age communities, we also need a term to describe elements of cultural continuity linking these communities with the early medieval period. Traditionally, this commonality has been described as Celtic and there is virtue in continuing to do so. As a consequence, there is every reason to think of the themes described in this book in terms of the emergence of 'Celtic Wales'.

6 Celtic Myths of Wales

The medieval mythic literature of Wales is a rich palimpsest of material wherein an amalgam of Christianity and paganism is present. In these prose tales, the earthworld of humans interacts seamlessly with the supernatural realms inhabited by spirit-forces, and miraculous occurrences are intermeshed with descriptions of noble families, human relationships and warfare. The earliest mythic texts – the *Pedeir Keinc y Mabinogi* (*The Four Branches of the Mabinogi*) and *Culhwch ac Olwen*, for instance – illustrate literary constructions that may well have had their genesis in oral tradition which, in turn, may have drawn ultimately upon inspirations from pre-Christian religious perceptions and beliefs. It is generally agreed (see p. 104) that the Welsh medieval mythic tales were compiled in written form within a Christian, monastic context. The texts thus contain a multifaceted collage, wherein broadly Christian ethics are punctuated by supranatural, pagan images which, despite their early origins, were perhaps – sometimes at least – specially selected by the authors of the texts in order to convey Christian morals and values.

Storytelling and the mythic tradition

A fundamental question to be raised in any enquiry concerning the early 'mythic' literature of Wales (and Ireland) pertains to its status as literary text. Were the stories related in the *Four Branches* or in *Culhwch ac Olwen* primal literature or were they essentially oral tales that were only later compiled in written form or were they originally designed as literature, which was subsequently utilized as story material?

Current scholarly opinion is that early Welsh 'mythic' tales were part of the stock-in-trade of the professional storyteller, the *cyfarwydd*. The stories, as presented in the surviving medieval literature, arguably had their genesis in an oral tradition that may belong to a much earlier period than the texts themselves. However, it is also clear, from their structure and the use of literary devices and formulae, that the written narratives were not simply the result of the dictation of oral tales to scribes but were constructed to be performed. At one and the same time, the stories encapsulate the oral techniques used by the *cyfarwydd* and are themselves examples of literary performance by the authors of the written texts. This is indicated by the use of conventions and literary devices, such as episodic structure, repetition, tripartism, direct and indirect speech. These 'tricks of the trade' are demonstrative of the dual character of medieval Welsh mythic texts: they were designed as literature but also reflect the oral performance of the professional storyteller or bard.

Storytellers, over the centuries, would have quarried the rich fund of oral material, selected, pruned, adapted and rationalized it to suit the needs of courtly entertainment. However, when the stories were written down, it is likely that particular individuals constructed the texts, not as reportage, but as deliberately structured literature. So we should view the *Four Branches* and, perhaps, also *Culhwch ac Olwen* as written tales which, in addition to their intrinsic interest, possess the bonus of presenting a 'window' on early medieval Wales, in much the same way as the early historical Irish mythic tradition, exemplified by the *Táin Bó Cuailnge*, is understood by scholars of Insular literature to be a window on early medieval Ireland.

The Four Branches of the Mabinogi

The *Four Branches of the Mabinogi* form a cohesive group within a larger body of eleven medieval prose tales, which are frequently known by the collective title *The Mabinogion*, after its first use by Lady Charlotte Guest in the mid-nineteenth century, when she translated the stories from Welsh into English. The eleven tales consist of the *Four Branches, Culhwch and Olwen, The Lady of the Fountain, Peredur, Geraint, The Encounter of Lludd and Llefelys, The Dream of Macsen* and *The Dream of Rhonabwy*.

For present purposes, it is appropriate to concentrate on the *Four Branches*, for these four tales are generally thought to be among the earliest written stories in *The Mabinogion*, the first recension (version) probably dating to around AD 1050–1120. The earliest surviving complete manuscripts of the *Four Branches* are contained within the *Llyfr Gwyn Rhydderch, c.* AD 1350 (the *White Book of Rhydderch*) and the *Llyfr Coch Hergest* (the *Red Book of Hergest*), *c.* 1400. If the tales are built upon an earlier foundation of oral narrative, then the eleventh-century origins of the written body of material might be capable of being pushed back several centuries further, perhaps to the period of interface between paganism and Christianity.

The tone or timbre of the *Four Branches* differs markedly from the cognate, and broadly coeval, Irish mythic tradition inasmuch as the Welsh texts contain repeated references to God, whereas such allusions are absent in the Irish prose tales, such as the *Táin*. However, both traditions may well have been composed as literature within a Christian clerical milieu. As was the case in early historical Ireland, the monasteries were highly influential foci of scholarship in early medieval Wales. Christian ethics are clearly present in the *Four Branches*: virtue, honour, chastity and goodness are emphasized; cheats, murderers and thieves all pay for their misdeeds.

Who wrote the Mabinogion?

Although attempts have been made to assign authorship of the *Four Branches* to particular individuals (notably Sulien, bishop of Saint David's or his son Rhigyfarch), the question remains unresolved. In her book, *The Four Branches of the Mabinogi*, Sioned Davies has rightly pointed out that, in medieval times, writing would have been the preserve of a relatively small number of scholars: clerics but also those educated by clerics. So, despite its Christian tone, the written narrative need not actually have been composed by a clergyman. What does seem clear, from the texts themselves, is that the cohesive and coherent character of the *Four Branches* makes it highly likely that the whole text was the work of a single scholastic author.

The *Four Branches* have no individual titles, although modern parlance has labelled them according to one of the principal characters in each Branch. Thus, though convenient, the nomenclature of 'Pwyll', 'Branwen', 'Manawydan' and 'Math' have no authenticity and, arguably, should not be used in modern discussions of the tales.

The First Branch relates the tale of Pwyll, the lord of Llys Arberth (Narberth), his wife Rhiannon and their son Pryderi. The first episode is built around the encounter – while out hunting –

Stone relief-carving of the Gaulish horse-goddess Epona, from Kastel, Germany. Epona was venerated all over Europe during the Roman period, from Scotland to Bulgaria. Max. width 25cm.

between Pwyll and Arawn, the lord of the Otherworld (Annwfn). Pwyll offends the honour code of the hunt, by inciting his own hounds to take Arawn's stag from the dogs of Annwfn. In atonement for this breach of etiquette, Pwyll agrees to change places and identities with Arawn for a year and, at the end of his sojourn in Annwfn, to kill Arawn's enemy Hafgan. It is interesting that the power of this lord of the Otherworld is insufficient to slay a fellow supernatural being; the flesh-and-blood potency of a human being is required to perform this task. (Such a state of affairs bears a strong resemblance to an occurrence in the Ulster Cycle of Irish medieval prose tales, where the young hero Cú Chulainn is enticed to the Otherworld by a supernatural being, in order to fulfil a particular task that can only be undertaken by someone from the world of humans.) The other important incident in this initial episode of the First Branch concerns Pwyll's behaviour whilst dwelling in Annwfn: although – in the physical guise of Arawn – he shares a bed with Arawn's wife, not wishing to cuckold her husband, he refuses to have intercourse with her. The second episode is the account of Pwyll's wooing and marriage to Rhiannon. After a three-year period of barrenness, Rhiannon produces a son, but he disappears on the third night after his birth. Rhiannon is framed for his murder by her watchwomen who, having fallen asleep while on guard over the child, kill a puppy and smear the queen's face and hands with its blood. The details of this framing are curious, for they seem to imply that Rhiannon is to be implicated not simply in infanticide but also in cannibalism. This being so, the penance imposed on her by Pwyll, for her alleged crime, is bizarre: she has to act as a beast of burden and carry visitors on her back from the horseblock outside the gates up to the *llys*. The scene now shifts to the house of one Teyrnon, lord of Gwent Iscoed, and the puzzling events of May-eve, when – every year – Teyrnon loses his newborn foal. One such night, Teyrnon keeps watch and, seeing a monstrous claw reach in through the stable window to grasp the foal, jumps forward and hacks off the great arm. (Readers of the Anglo-Saxon epic poem *Beowulf* will see a close parallel between this incident and that of the monster, Grendel, who terrorizes the Danish royal house, prowling round the court at night and grabbing young warriors when they are sleeping; the youthful visiting hero, Beowulf, stands watch for Grendel and wrenches off his arm while wrestling with him.) As Teyrnon lops off the arm and saves his foal, there is a commotion outside the stable and investigation of its source reveals a baby, wrapped in a silk shawl, deposited on the threshold. Teyrnon and his wife adopt the infant as their foster-son, and the child, by his remarkable precocity, soon betrays his special, heroic, status. When he is four years old, his foster-parents realize that he must be the lost child of Pwyll and Rhiannon, and he is reunited with his birth-parents, his mother naming him Pryderi ('Worry' or 'Care') because he has been lost for so long.

The Second Branch focuses upon the family of Llŷr in Harlech and, in particular, on Brân (Bendigeidfran) and his sister Branwen. The story begins with the engagement of Branwen to Matholwch, king of Ireland. Branwen's half-brother Efnisien is incensed by this betrothal and displays his resentment by mutilating the horses belonging to Matholwch and his retinue, the grossest of insults to a royal guest. Brân hastens to mollify his sister's betrothed by showering prestigious gifts upon him, the most significant of such presents being a magical cauldron of regeneration: in it, dead warriors, cooked overnight, are resurrected next day, as good as new save that they cannot speak (a metaphor for their belonging to the Otherworld, and one which is repeated in the enchantment of Pryderi and Rhiannon, in the Third Branch). Seemingly appeased by Brân's gifts, Matholwch takes his bride home to Ireland and the couple produce a son, Gwern. But, thereafter, Branwen begins to pay the price for Efnisien's insult and she is continually abused, beaten and humiliated, and forced to work in the kitchens as a servant. Although care is taken that no word of Branwen's treatment should reach her brother, she manages to train a starling to take Brân a message, and he musters a British (Welsh) army to rescue her. Efnisien accompanies the host, and his destructive character re-emerges when he tosses Matholwch's son Gwern into the fire. In a bitter twist of irony, Brân's gift of the cauldron to the Irish king threatens the downfall of the donor's forces inasmuch as Matholwch is using the vessel to recycle his dead warriors to set against the army of Britain. But Efnisien finally redeems himself: he jumps into the cauldron and bursts it asunder. Britain wins the battle but it is a Pyrrhic victory; nearly everyone is slain. Of Harlech's army, only seven survive; Brân is mortally wounded by a poisoned spear. He commands his depleted band to behead him; after sojourning with the head for some years at Harlech and Gwales, Brân's men finally inter it in London, facing east, in accordance with their leader's last instruction. Incidentally, during the long time span between Brân's decapitation and the burial of his head in London, it remains whole and uncorrupted.

The enchantment of Dyfed is the theme of the Third Branch. Following the death of Pwyll, Pryderi gives his mother Rhiannon as a wife to Manawydan. After feasting at Llys Arberth, the pair of them go up to the Gorsedd Arberth (the same magical place from which Pwyll first set eyes on Rhiannon), accompanied by Pryderi and his wife Cigfa. As they gaze over the land, Dyfed disappears in a spell-wrought mist. The two men set off with their wives to find employment in England; here, Manawydan (a magician) excites envy and hostility wherever he settles, because he excels at every craft he tries, thereby putting his rivals out of business. On their return to Dyfed, Manawydan and Pryderi go off hunting, and have an encounter with the supernatural, in the form of a huge white boar, which lures Pryderi and his dogs to a strange castle or *caer*. Once inside the mysterious building, Pryderi falls under the enchantment of a golden bowl, a *cawg*; as he touches it, he becomes frozen to the spot, unable to move or speak. When Rhiannon finds him, she too falls under the spell.

Bereft of his hunting-dogs, Manawydan turns from the chase to agriculture, and cultivates three fields of wheat. The crops grow strong and true but, as Manawydan prepares to harvest each of the first two fields in turn, so the corn is destroyed by an army of mice. Manawydan watches over the third field and catches the last mouse, slower than the rest, for she is pregnant. There follows a bizarre episode in which Manawydan makes preparations to hang the captive mouse, and is interrupted by a bishop who tries to redeem the animal. Recognizing the man as a magician (like himself), Manawydan demands the restoration of Dyfed in return for the release of the mouse. The bishop reveals himself as Llwyd and confesses that it was he who cast the spell on the land, in revenge for the wrong done, long ago, by Pwyll when he cheated Rhiannon's first suitor, Gwawl, of his bride. The mouse-prisoner is Llwyd's wife, whom Llwyd has sent with her companions in mouse-form to ravage Manawydan's crops. The collapse of Llwyd's magic frees Dyfed, along with Rhiannon and Pryderi.

The Fourth Branch is set in Gwynedd, among the dynasty of Dôn. The principal characters are Math, lord of Gwynedd, his nephew Gwydion, his sister Arianrhod, her son Lleu and his fickle wife, Blodeuwedd. Math himself has a curious 'bond' (Irish *geis*) or injunction on him: unless at war, he must sit with his feet in a virgin's lap. At first glance, such a strange feature is inexplicable, but it may relate to symbolism associated with sacral kingship, similar to the myth of sovereignty present in cognate Irish literature, wherein there is an essential union between the king and the personified land. The virgin footholder, with her undissipated sexuality, may represent the personification of sovereignty and the fertility of the land. Gwydion's brother Gilfaethwy falls in love with Math's footholder, Goewin; he and his brother conspire to release her from Math's service by fomenting war with a southern Welsh chiefdom. Math goes to war and Pryderi, a leader of the opposing force, is slain. Goewin is seduced by Gilfaethwy; Math's fury, when he returns, causes him to put a spell on the brothers, turning them – for three consecutive years – into gendered pairs of different wild animals: a stag and hind, a boar and sow and a wolf and she-wolf.

The next episode in the Fourth Branch concerns candidacy for the now vacant position of footholder. Gwydion's sister Arianrhod applies, but Math has devised a test of purity, involving a requirement to step over his magical staff, and Arianrhod fails the test – spectacularly so – by giving birth to two boys. The first child, Dylan, quickly fades from the scene, but the second infant becomes the central character of this final episode. Arianrhod places three curses or prohibitions on the baby (some scholars have speculated that Arianrhod's aversion to her son arises from his incestuous conception following the illicit union between her and her brother Gwydion): first that he shall be nameless unless his mother names him; second that he shall be not be armed unless she herself equips him; thirdly that he shall have no mortal wife. These *geissi* are significant in that each curse represents denial of a crucial rite of passage for a young male's attainment of manhood. The child's uncle, Gwydion, uses his powers as a magician in order to trick Arianrhod into naming him Lleu Llaw Gyffes (the Bright One of the Skilful Hand) and arming him; Math and Gwydion between them conjure a wife for him, Blodeuwedd.

The false woman of flowers

Lleu's wife is conjured out of three wild flowers: oak, broom and meadowsweet, and this gives rise to her name Blodeuwedd ('Flower Woman'). Blodeuwedd's magical origin means that she is rootless and, therefore, amoral; she is unfaithful to Lleu and conspires with her lover, Gronw, to murder him. But, as Lleu is struck the mortal blow, he is transformed into an eagle, and is subsequently rescued and restored to human form by Gwydion, who kills Gronw. Blodeuwedd – not being mortal – cannot be destroyed but she is punished by being condemned to eternal life in the form of an owl, a solitary creature of the darkness.

The *Four Branches* are, at one and the same time, cohesive yet distinct, one from the other. Characters recur from Branch to Branch: Rhiannon and Pryderi are good examples. Episodes are also linked: thus Llwyd, the enchanter of Dyfed in the Third Branch, refers to an incident which took place in the First (Pwyll's dishonourable behaviour towards Rhiannon's original suitor, Gwawl). Yet each tale also stands alone. Within each Branch, the punctuation of the storyline into distinct episodes is an illustration of the conventions of literary and narrative performance. The switching of tenses, the use of direct and reported speech, repetition and tripartism (the three fields of corn, the three years of Math's curse on his nephews, the description of Branwen as one of three fairest women exemplify this formulaic feature) all contribute to the professional storyteller's 'grammar' of performance.

The essentially mythic nature of the *Four Branches* is characterized by the strong thread of supernatural occurrences that are present in each of the Branches. Such incidents are far too numerous to mention them all, but a few examples will suffice to demonstrate their centrality. In the First Branch, Pwyll spends a year in the Otherworld, described as if it were a mirror-image of all that is most enjoyable in earthly life, although the inhabitants of this world do not possess all the faculties of humans (hence Arawn's need for Pwyll to kill Hafgan). Pwyll's meeting with Rhiannon is hedged about with mystery: he sees her when he is in a special location, Gorsedd Arberth, where strange things tend to happen; she appears to him on a dazzling white horse and, try as he might, neither he nor his swiftest horsemen can catch up with her, despite her leisurely pace. Brân, hero of the Second Branch, is described as too large for any house to contain him; he is so tall that he can wade effortlessly across the Irish Sea. His gift to Matholwch is a magical cauldron that allows dead warriors to be restored, albeit as voiceless zombies. The whole of the Third Branch is redolent with the paranormal: Dyfed vanishes in a mist; a magical *caer* suddenly appears, and the golden *cawg* inside it holds those who touch it literally spellbound; women shape-shift and become destructive mice. The Fourth Branch is similarly based almost wholly on supernatural beings and occurrences: metamorphosis is a dominant theme and involves Gwydion (both as victim of a shape-shifting curse and as perpetrator of transformation of others), Gilfaethwy, Lleu and Blodeuwedd (herself a supernatural creation).

Taken at face value, the *Four Branches* present the audience with an intricate and exciting set of 'fairy tales'. If this façade is peeled away, a sophisticated, consciously structured and elaborate piece of 'oral literature' is revealed which arguably contains both Christian ethics and resonances of a pagan past, the latter – perhaps – playing an important rôle in legitimizing the present.

Culhwch ac Olwen

The story of Culhwch is the earliest of the Arthurian prose tales and may be even earlier, in its first written compilation, than the *Four Branches*, perhaps dating to around AD 1100. *Culhwch ac Olwen* is essentially a quest tale or, more accurately, a quest-within-a-quest. The central theme is Culhwch's search for Olwen, a girl he has never seen. In brief, the story concerns the young nobleman Culhwch, a cousin of Arthur and the son of Cilydd and Goleuddyd. On the death of his wife, Culhwch's father remarries; his new partner has a grown-up daughter whom she wishes Culhwch to wed. When he demurs (pleading his extreme youth), she curses him, with the promise that the only woman he will marry is Olwen, the daughter of the fearsome giant Ysbaddaden. The mere mention of Olwen's name by his step-mother is enough to make Culhwch fall violently in love with her, and he sets off to Arthur's court to enlist his help in the search for his bride. After a year of seeking Olwen, they eventually find her, but now Culhwch faces a further hurdle, in that Olwen's father Ysbaddaden is under a *geis* (an early Irish word meaning injunction or bond) wherein his daughter's marriage will presage his death. He therefore applies virtually impossible conditions for Culhwch to fulfil before he will agree to Olwen's wedding: he must perform a range of superhuman tasks (very reminiscent of the Labours of Hercules). The greatest of Culhwch's tasks is the capture of a great, enchanted boar – Twrch Trwyth, transformed by God for his great wickedness – and the retrieval of the scissors, razor and comb from between the creature's ears (the inner quest of the tale). After a long chase over south Wales, Cornwall and Ireland, the boar is subdued, the toilet-articles handed over to Ysbaddaden and the marriage of Culhwch and Olwen takes place.

Like the *Four Branches*, *Culhwch ac Olwen* contains a pervading element of the supernatural. Culhwch's destiny is inextricably linked with pigs: the circumstances of his birth, amongst a herd of swine, his consequent naming 'Culhwch' (Pig Run) and the quest for Twrch Trwyth all demonstrate this close linkage. Culhwch himself has significant supernatural powers: when he arrives at the court of Arthur unannounced, he is denied entry by the gate-keeper and, in his rage at this insult, the young man threatens to utter three shouts that will cause any pregnant woman in the land to abort her foetus and that will make all other women barren. Such an episode may be a metaphoric device to signify Culhwch's god-like power to make the land infertile. Later, when Arthur's warband sallies forth to find Olwen, the cousins enlist the help of Mabon the Hunter, the son of Modron. These two characters are barely disguised divinities: Mabon (The Youth) is paradoxically described as the oldest living creature in the world; Modron (Mother) may be an archetypal mother-goddess figure. Mabon's name is cognate with that of Maponus, a deity recorded on inscriptions from the north of Roman Britain and central Gaul. The whole tale is permeated by transmogrification or shape-shifting. Twrch Trwyth confides that he and his followers have been transformed to pigs by God for their wicked ways. In the quest for Olwen, Arthur, Culhwch and Mabon enlist the aid of a whole series of magical animals with whom Arthur's man Gwrhyr is able to converse. Both Mabon and another god – Gofannon the Smith – have Irish divine counterparts: Oenghus, the Young Man and Goibnhiu, the blacksmith-god of Insular myth.

Two cauldron myths

Two early medieval Welsh texts, outside the eleven tales of the *Mabinogion* are of particular interest, in terms of their mythic content; both stories are woven around cauldrons with supernatural properties. One is *Preiddeu Annwfn*, a poem which recounts a disastrous raiding expedition made by Arthur to Annwfn to plunder its magical cauldron. The second is the tale of Ceridwen's Cauldron.

The *Book of Taliesin*, named after the great sixth-century Welsh satire-poet, contains a tale concerning the euhemerized (that is a divinized historical character) Taliesin himself, and narrates the story of a supernatural 'cauldron of poesy', a vessel which imparted wisdom and inspiration. The keeper of the cauldron was a sorceress named Ceridwen; she had two children, a comely girl, Crearwy, and a hideous son, Afagddu. In order to compensate the latter for his appearance, his mother brewed a magical potion to make Afagddu all-knowing and infinitely wise. The concoction had to be boiled for a year before it was ready for consumption, and Ceridwen gave the job of looking after the cauldron and its steaming contents to a young boy, Gwion. By 'chance', three drops of the scalding broth spattered onto Gwion's hand and, by instinctively licking his sore fingers, Gwion unwittingly became the unintended recipient of the cauldron's wisdom. The vessel then

One of a pair of sheet-bronze cauldrons from the votive lake-deposit at Llyn Fawr, Glamorgan; eighth to seventh century BC. Cauldrons like these were prestigious possessions, used in ceremonial feasting and ritual, and occur throughout the Iron Age and into the Roman period.

burst wide open and the rest of the potion was lost; the furious Ceridwen pursued Gwion, changing both of them into different animals – hunter and prey – as the chase proceeded. She became first a greyhound, and Gwion a hare; in the form of an otter she chased the boy (who had become a fish); he was then transformed into a small bird, pursued by Ceridwen as a hawk. In the final metamorphosis, Ceridwen changed herself into a hen and swallowed the grain of corn that Gwion had become. After nine months, she gave birth to a baby boy, Gwion reborn. Still angry, Ceridwen was prepared to kill the infant, but could not bring herself to destroy so beautiful a child. So – like Moses in his basket – he was set adrift in a coracle. He was found, floating in the water, by Elphin, a courtier of King Maelgwn (a sixth-century historical king) and was given the name Taliesin (Radiant Brow). The boy grew up to become the most prominent satirist, poet and prophet in the land.

The shape-shifting engendered by Ceridwen in the tale reflects a repetitive and dominant device which is common to both Welsh

The cauldron of Annwfn

Preiddeu Annwfn (The Spoils of Annwfn) is an early medieval Welsh text, probably of thirteenth-century date (or earlier); it is preserved in the *Book of Taliesin*. The piece has an interesting connection with *Culhwch ac Olwen* inasmuch as both stories contain references to Arthur as a 'cauldron-rustler'. In *Culhwch*, one of the 'impossible' tasks the eponymous hero has to perform is the obtention of the cauldron of Diwrnach the Irishman, 'to boil meat for thy wedding guests' says Ysbaddaden. The vessel is brought back by Arthur, filled with the treasures of Ireland, after a successful but bitterly contested raid. The focus of *Preiddeu Annwfn* is Arthur's plundering of the Otherworld for its valuable cauldron, a vessel studded with precious stones and possessing a distinct, and decidedly capricious, persona: it requires the breath of nine virgins to heat the liquid inside it, and it flatly refuses to boil food for a coward. Arthur's expedition is successful but only at immense human cost; he loses nearly all his ships and forces in the raid. Such a Pyrrhic victory outcome to battles is something which occurs also in the *Four Branches* and in *Culhwch*. It may be that, in the context of literary composition by Christian clergy, the message conveyed by such tales has overtones of morality and Christian ethics, in which disapproval of war for gain is expressed. The same idea seems to be present in early Irish mythic texts, such as the *Táin Bó Cuailnge*, which is – again – woven through with (disguised) Christian moral issues and, in particular, discouragement of cattle-raiding.

and Irish mythic literature, where it serves as an indicator of supernatural agency. Additionally, the features ascribed to Ceridwen's cauldron bear a striking resemblance to the *peir* in *Preiddeu Annwfn*, inasmuch as each vessel has a definite persona and – to some extent – participates actively in the development of the storyline. Thus, the cauldron of Annwfn chooses for whom it will consent to cook food, just as Ceridwen's vessel possesses a will of its own and defies her by selecting Gwion/Taliesin as the receptor of its brew of knowledge rather than Afagddu and then destroying itself after the magical potion is ingested by Gwion, so that no part of its contents can be recovered.

114

The cauldron-symbolism in the Welsh myths, wherein regeneration, plenty and destruction are paradoxically juxtaposed, is highly reminiscent of the ambiguous Otherworld cauldrons of the Irish mythic tradition. The description of cauldrons in secular Welsh medieval documents, such as the Laws of Hywel Dda, is interesting, for they are clearly high-status containers, associated with royalty and nobility. One of the laws, dealing with the division of property between men and women, makes it clear that cauldrons were not simply part of everyday household cooking-equipment, for they were allocated to males of high rank rather than to women. The notion of cauldrons as prestige objects, which is implicit in the Welsh myths, is endorsed by the archaeological evidence for cauldrons as important ritual containers. From the later Bronze Age through to the early post-Roman period in Ireland, Britain (particularly Wales and Scotland) and Europe, cauldrons were deposited in lakes, rivers and marshes as votive gifts, sometimes filled with metalwork, or as grave-goods in tombs.

Recurrent mythic themes and conventions

Within the early medieval mythic literature considered in this chapter, it is possible to identify a number of repeated thematic devices that appear to be part of the regular repertoire of the storytellers or authors who recounted or compiled the tales. An important feature is triplism (or tripartism), the dominance of the number three. Thus, in the First Branch of the Mabinogi, Rhiannon's baby, Pryderi, disappears on the third night of his

The horse-symbolism of Rhiannon

Rhiannon has a close link with horses, inasmuch as she first appears to Pwyll on horseback; her penance for the alleged murder of her son is to act like a horse or donkey; and this horse-symbolism is picked up again in the Third Branch, where Rhiannon's enchantment – after touching the *cawg* – involves her wearing the halter of an ass. In fact, the perceived connection between Rhiannon and horses is so marked that some scholars believe she is a manifestation of the Roman-period Gaulish horse-goddess Epona.

birth; in the Second Branch, Branwen is described as one of the three fairest women in the land; later in the same tale, Brân's followers encounter the three magical singing birds of Rhiannon. In the Third Branch, Manawydan plants three fields of corn; in the Fourth, Math turns his nephews into three sets of wild beasts; Arianrhod imposes three *geissi* (curses) on her baby son. In *Culhwch*, the boy threatens to shout three times at Arthur's gate if not admitted to his cousin's presence; in *Preiddeu Annwfn*, multiples of three are present in the nine virgins, whose breath heats the cauldron. Triplism is not only also important in the broadly coeval Insular myths but it features prominently, too, in the pre-Christian cult iconography of western Europe in, for example, sculptural depictions of the three mother-goddesses, triple-horned bulls and boars and triple-headed images. It is possible, that the tripartism present in these mythic texts may contain resonances of this much earlier religious structure, particularly if oral tradition did play a significant role in feeding into the literary composition of the tales.

The close linkages between humans and animals are another recurrent device in the Welsh mythic repertoire. Animals play a particularly pivotal role in the *Four Branches* and in *Culhwch ac Olwen*. Certain beasts, such as boars and stags, appear to facilitate or enable associations between the world of humans and the realms of the supernatural: thus, in the First Branch, a stag-hunt sets the stage for the encounter between Pwyll and Arawn, lord of the Otherworld. In the Third Branch, a great white boar lures Manawydan's hunting-dogs to the enchanted *caer*; pigs are again central to the *Culhwch* myth, both in the circumstances of his birth and in his quest for Twrch Trwyth.

Dogs are also significant in the tales: hunting-dogs enable encounters with the Otherworld: in the First Branch, Pwyll's hounds meet those of Arawn, and these infernal creatures are strange to look at: they are white, with red ears (precisely the appearance of Otherworld animals in some of the Irish myths). Shape-shifting between human and animal-form is another illustration of the close linkage between people and beasts: transmogrification is particularly prominent in the Fourth Branch, where Gwydion, Gilfaethwy and Blodeuwedd each suffer this as a punishment (as does Twrch Trwyth, in *Culhwch*). Lleu shape-shifts to the form of an eagle but, on this occasion, it occurs as a means of preserving his life. Transformation also occurs in the story of Ceridwen's pursuit of Gwion. Finally, in looking at the roles of animals and humans, we should recall the ability of Arthur's man Gwrhyr to use speech to enlist the help of a variety of fantastic creatures: the Salmon of Llyn Llyw, the Stag of Rhedynfre and other weird and wonderful beasts.

The quest for Arthur

A powerful literary theme is Arthur and Camelot. From Malory to Disney and beyond, Arthur still fascinates. But the 'historical' Arthur is a shadowy figure with only limited evidence for his historicity. Nevertheless, the balance of probability is that there once was an Arthur. Particularly important are two marginal entries in an Easter Annal, now held in the British Library, which ends with the death of Rhodri ap Hywel Dda. The entry for AD 518 describes the Battle of Badon where Arthur 'carried the cross of our Lord Jesus Christ' and defeated the Saxons. The entry for AD 539 notes the death of Arthur in 'the strife of Camlann'. Later Welsh evidence may also be significant: the *Gododdin*, for example, describes the warrior Gwawrddur who, while heroic, 'was not Arthur'. A spate of young princelings appeared in several Welsh kingdoms in about AD 600; the sudden popularity of the name for these young noblemen may point to an early warrior hero called Arthur, who perhaps adopted the title *dux bellorum* when fighting against the Saxons. Many parts of Britain have laid claim to this Arthur and Wales has its strong candidates. Indeed, some tales of the *Mabinogi* are quite specific: Arthur, we are told, 'was in his chief court at Caer Llion ar Wysg'. Unfortunately, such references are coloured by the highly imaginative writings of Geoffrey of Monmouth and, in truth, there is no hard evidence to link Arthur with any identifiable site. It is interesting to speculate, however, that a mobile cavalry leader might be attracted to a prominent location such as the former legionary fortress as a rallying-point. It is impossible to assign Arthur to any location, but as compelling a case can be made for Caerleon as for anywhere else.

The Welsh mythic texts present a kaleidoscopic picture of intertwined paganism and Christianity, with the pagan elements gaining the upper hand. The Otherworld is a transparently pagan device (although – perhaps – with undertones of the Christian heaven), as are the superhuman features of Brân, Gwydion and Rhiannon. Mabon and Modron in *Culhwch* are thinly disguised divinities: the archetypal Mother and Son, such as are familiar from such myths as that of the ancient Phrygian god and goddess Atys and Cybele. Shape-changing, cauldrons of regeneration (which, however, remind us irresistibly of the two New Testament episodes of loaves and fishes), uncorrupted heads, enchantments and spells all belong to an essentially pagan world. But Christianity also plays an overt part in the stories. References to God are made, for instance, in Twrch Trwyth's explanation of his transformed state. It is possible also, as we have seen, to identify definite ethical messages in the manner in which several episodes in the tales develop; honesty, integrity and chastity are championed; nefarious behaviour is avenged; fidelity in women is praised, adultery condemned. Warfare, and especially cattle-raiding are negative activities; generosity and compassion are rewarded. In fact, it is easier to imagine Christian authorship of these Welsh mythic tales than is the case with the broadly contemporaneous Irish prose stories, although here – too – Christianity is covertly present.

Archaeology and myth: connections or coincidence?

There appear to be certain close linkages between themes in the medieval Welsh myths and aspects of the material culture of western Europe belonging to the Iron Age and Roman periods. If these connections are genuine rather than coincidental, it is necessary to postulate the mechanisms by which this could have occurred, particularly if we bear in mind the long time-gap between – say – the last few centuries BC and the eleventh century AD. If the myths do contain a legacy from the pre-Christian past, it may be that such resonances came about through oral tradition, in which transmission of information and memory, perceptions about religion and ritual practice and the supernatural world might have taken place over centuries. An alternative, or additional, model is one in which early Christian clerics, the literary composers or redactors of the myths, or the storytellers whose repertoire of tales fed into the literature, may actually have observed (or talked to those who had observed) elements of ancient material culture which visibly survived in the landscape.

118

We know, for example, that some of the early Irish monks, like Columbanus in the sixth century, travelled long distances within Britain and Europe. Such peripatetic clerics or storytellers, seeing preserved monuments, such as altars carved with images of Roman date, may have been influenced by what they saw and – consciously or unconsciously – have woven these images into their stories. Thus, a medieval Welsh author may have observed carvings of Epona, the horse-goddess, and have been inspired by what he witnessed, in terms of the construction of Rhiannon's persona. In the same way, ancient cauldrons, deposited in lakes or marshes, may have been discovered by chance by people fishing or reed-cutting and the circumstances of their finds relayed to storytellers or writers. Such a model may appear far-fetched but Giraldus Cambrensis, writing in the late twelfth century, commented on the remains of Roman Caerleon that he observed on his journey through Wales. Gerald's account makes it clear that, in his day, certain monuments of Roman date were both highly visible within the landscape and – in some cases – virtually intact. It is our contention that 'ancestral voices' may be relevant to the myths of Wales and that what we may be seeing in this literature is, in a sense, a discourse between pasts, those of the medieval period, on the one hand, and of much earlier times, on the other.

Further Reading

Leslie Alcock, *Dinas Powys: An Iron Age, Dark Age and Early Medieval Settlement in Glamorgan* Cardiff: National Museum of Wales, 1963.

Leslie Alcock, *Economy, Society and Warfare among the Britons and Saxons* Cardiff: University of Wales Press, 1987.

Kevin Blockley, *Prestatyn 1984–5: An Iron Age Farmstead and Romano-British Industrial Settlement in North Wales* Oxford: British Archaeological Reports no. 210, 1989.

George C. Boon (ed.), *Monographs and Collections. I. Roman Sites* Cardiff: Cambrian Archaeological Association, 1978.

George C. Boon, *The Legionary Fortress of Caerleon-Isca* Cardiff: National Museum of Wales, 1987.

Kenneth Brassil, 'Early Celtic art', in S. Aldhouse-Green (ed.), *Explaining the Unexplainable: Art, Ritual and Death in Prehistory* Cardiff: National Museums & Galleries of Wales, 1996, pp.26–8.

Richard J. Brewer, *Corpus Signorum Imperii Romani. Great Britain Vol. I, Fasc. 5, Wales* London/Oxford: British Academy/Oxford University Press, 1986.

Richard J. Brewer, *Caerleon-Isca* Cardiff: National Museum of Wales, 1987.

Barry Burnham and Jeffery L. Davies (eds.), *Conquest, Co-Existence and Change: Recent Work in Roman Wales* Lampeter: *Trivium* no. 25, 1991.

P. John Casey (ed.), *The End of Roman Britain* Oxford University Press, 1979.

P. John Casey, *Carausius and Allectus: The British Usurpers* London: Batsford, 1994.

P. John Casey and Jeffery L. Davies, *Excavations at Segontium (Caernarfon) Roman Fort, 1975–1979* Council for British Archaeology, 1993.

Simon Esmonde Cleary, *The Ending of Roman Britain* London: Batsford, 1989.

Bryony Coles, John Coles and Mogens Schou Jorgensen (eds.), *Bog Bodies, Sacred Sites and Wetland Archaeology* Exeter: Wetland Archaeology Research Project Occasional Paper 12, 1999.

John Collis, 'The origin and spread of the Celts', *Studia Celtica* 30 (1996), 17–34.

Barry Cunliffe, *The Ancient Celts* Oxford: Oxford University Press, 1997.

Ken Dark, *Civitas to Kingdom: British Political Continuity 300–800* Leicester University Press, 1994.

Ken Dark, *Discovery by Design: The Identification of Secular Elite Settlements in Western Britain AD 400–700* Oxford: British Archaeological Reports, 1994.

Ken and Petra Dark, *The Landscape of Roman Britain* Stroud: Alan Sutton, 1997.

Elwyn Davies, *A Gazetteer of Welsh Place-Names* Cardiff: University of Wales Press, 1975.

Jeffery L. Davies, 'Roman military deployment in Wales and the Marches from Claudius to the Antonines', in W. S. Hanson and L. J. F. Keppie (eds.), *Roman Frontier Studies 1979* Oxford: British Archaeological Reports no. 71, 1980, pp.255–77.

Jeffery L. Davies, 'The Early Celts in Wales', in Miranda J. Green (ed.), *The Celtic World*, pp.671–700.

Oliver Davies, *Celtic Christianity in Early Medieval Wales* Cardiff: University of Wales Press, 1996.

Sioned Davies, *The Four Branches of the Mabinogi. Pedeir Keinc y Mabinogi* Llandysul: Gomer Press, 1993.

Sioned Davies, *Crefft y Cyfarwydd: Astudiaeth o Dechnegau Naratif yn y Mabinogion* Cardiff: University of Wales Press, 1995.

Wendy Davies, *Wales in the Early Middle Ages* Leicester University Press, 1982.

Wendy Davies, *Patterns of Power in Early Wales* Oxford University Press, 1990.

Nancy Edwards and Alan Lane, *Early Medieval Settlements in Wales AD 400–1100* Cardiff: Early Medieval Wales Research Group, 1988.

Nancy Edwards and Alan Lane (eds.), *The Early Church in Wales and the West* Oxford: Oxbow, 1992.

David Ellis Evans, 'The Early Celts: the evidence of language', in Miranda J. Green (ed.), *The Celtic World* pp.8–20.

David Ellis Evans, 'Celticity, Celtic awareness and Celtic studies', *Zeitschrift für Celtische Philologie* 49–50 (1997), 1–27.

David Ellis Evans, 'Linguistics and Celtic ethnogenesis', in Ronald Black, William Gillies and Roibeard Ó Maolalaigh (eds.), *Celtic Connections. Proceedings of the 10th International Congress of Celtic Studies* East Lothian: Tuckwell Press, 1999, pp.1–18.

Willoughby Gardner and Hubert Savory, *Dinorben: A Hillfort Occupied in Early Iron Age and Roman Times* Cardiff: National Museum of Wales, 1964.

Paul Graves-Brown, Siân Jones and Clive Gamble (eds.), *Cultural Identity and Archaeology* London: Routledge, 1996.

Miranda Green, *Dictionary of Celtic Myth and Legend* London: Thames & Hudson, 1992.

Miranda J. Green (ed.), *The Celtic World* London: Routledge, 1995.

Miranda Green, 'Introduction: Who were the Celts?', in Miranda J. Green (ed.), *The Celtic World* London: Routledge, 1995, pp.3–7.

Miranda Green, *Celtic Goddesses: Warriors, Virgins and Mothers* London: British Museum, 1995.

Miranda Green, 'Art and religion: aspects of identity in pagan Celtic Europe', *Studia Celtica* 30 (1996), 35–58.

Miranda Green, *Celtic Art: Reading the Messages* London: Weidenfeld & Nicolson, 1996.

Miranda Green, *Exploring the World of the Druids* London: Thames & Hudson, 1997.

Miranda Green, 'Back to the future: resonances of the past in myth and material culture', in Cornelius Holtorf and Amy Gazin-Schwartz (eds.), *Archaeology and Folklore* London: Routledge, 1999, pp.48–66.

Nicholas Higham, *Rome, Britain and the Anglo-Saxons* London: Seaby, 1992.

Gwilym Hughes, *The Excavation of a Late Prehistoric and Romano-British Settlement at Thornwell Farm, Chepstow* Oxford: British Archaeological Reports, no. 244, 1996.

Simon James, 'Celts, politics and motivation in archaeology', *Antiquity* 72 (1998), 200–9.

Simon James, *The Atlantic Celts: Ancient People or Modern Invention?* London: The British Museum Press, 1999.

Michael Jarrett and Stuart Wrathmell, *Whitton: An Iron Age and Roman Farmstead in South Glamorgan* Cardiff: University of Wales Press, 1981.

Gwyn Jones and Thomas Jones, *The Mabinogion* London: J. Dent, 1976.

Michael Jones, *The End of Roman Britain* Cornell University Press, 1998.

Siân Jones, *The Archaeology of Ethnicity* London: Routledge, 1997.

Brendan Lehane, *Early Celtic Christianity* London: John Constable, 1994.

M. Lloyd Jones, *Society and Settlement in Wales and the Marches 500 BC–AD 1100* Oxford: British Archaeological Reports, no. 121, 1984.

David Longley, 'Bryn Eryr: an enclosed settlement of the Iron Age on Anglesey', *Proceedings of the Prehistoric Society* 64 (1998), 225–73.

Frances Lynch, *Prehistoric Anglesey* (revised 2nd edition) Llangefni: The Anglesey Antiquarian Society, 1991.

James Mallory (ed.), *Aspects of the Táin* Belfast: Universities Press, 1992.

John Manley, S. Grenter and F. Gale, *The Archaeology of Clwyd* Mold: Clwyd County Council, 1991.

William H. Manning, *Report on the Excavations at Usk 1965–1976* (2 vols) Cardiff: University of Wales Press, 1981, 1989.

Ruth and Vincent Megaw, 'Do the ancient Celts still live? An essay in identity and contextuality', *Studia Celtica* 31 (1997), 107–24.

Donald Moore (ed.), *The Irish Sea Province in Archaeology and History* Cardiff: Cambrian Archaeological Association, 1970.

S. Moscati, Otto-Hermann Frey, Venceslas Kruta, Barry Raftery and M. Szabó (eds.), *The Celts* (Catalogue of an Exhibition at the Palazzo Grassi, Venice entitled *The Celts, the Origins of Europe*) London: Thames & Hudson, 1991.

Chris Musson, *The Breiddin Hillfort. A Later Prehistoric Settlement in the Welsh Marches* Council for British Archaeology Report no. 76/Cadw, 1991.

Joseph F. Nagy, *Conversing with Angels and Ancients. Literary Myths of Medieval Ireland* Dublin/New York: Four Courts Press/Cornell University Press, 1997.

V. E. Nash-Williams (2nd edition, M. G. Jarrett (ed.)), *The Roman Frontier in Wales* Cardiff: University of Wales Press, 1969.

National Museum of Wales, *Early Iron Age Art in Wales* Cardiff: National Museum of Wales, 1968.

Hywel Wyn Owen, *The Place-Names of Wales* Cardiff: University of Wales Press/The Western Mail, 1998.

Tim Potter and Catherine Johns, *Roman Britain* London: British Museum Press, 1992.

David Rankin, *Celts and the Classical World* London: Routledge, 1996.

Mark Redknap, *The Christian Celts: Treasures of Late Celtic Wales* Cardiff: National Museum of Wales, 1990.

David Robinson (ed.), *Biglis, Caldicot and Llandough. Three Late Iron Age and Romano-British Sites in South-East Wales. Excavations 1977–79* Oxford: British Archaeological Reports, no. 188, 1988.

Peter Salway, *Roman Britain* Oxford University Press, 1985.

Hubert Savory, *Guide Catalogue of the Early Iron Age Collections* Cardiff: National Museum of Wales, 1976.

Patrick Sims-Williams, 'Celtomania and Celtoscepticism', *Cambrian Medieval Celtic Studies* 36 (1998), 1–35.

C. Snyder, *Sub-Roman Britain (AD 400–600)* Oxford: British Archaeological Reports, no. 247, 1996.

Charles Thomas, *Christianity in Roman Britain to AD 500* London: Batsford, 1993.

Charles Thomas, *And Shall These Mute Stones Speak: Post-Roman Inscriptions in Western Britain* Cardiff: University of Wales Press. 1994.

Rick Turner and R. Scaife (eds.), *Bog Bodies. New Discoveries and New Perspectives* London: British Museum, 1995.

John Wacher, *The Towns of Roman Britain* London: Routledge, 1995.

Graham Webster, *Rome against Caratacus: The Roman Campaigns in Britain AD 48–58* London: Batsford, 1981.

Graham Webster (ed.), *Fortress into City: The Consolidation of Roman Britain* London: Batsford, 1988.

Peter V. Webster, 'The Roman period', in H. N. Savory (ed.), *Glamorgan County History Vol. II. Early Glamorgan* Cardiff: Glamorgan County History, 1984, pp.277–313.

George Williams, *Fighting and Farming in Iron Age West Wales: Excavations at Llawhaden 1980–1984* Dyfed Archaeological Trust & Manpower Services Commission, 1985.

Glossary

agape	Christian supper of 'friendly affection'
amphora	large Roman ceramic container for wine, oil or sauce
antefix	clay roofing-tile
anthropomorphic	in human form
auxiliary	non-citizen soldier in a Roman unit other than a legion
ballista	Roman military engine for hurling stones
basilica	town hall, usually attached to the forum in a Roman town
cantref	Welsh medieval territorial unit in theory made up of a hundred townships (*trefi*)
chthonic	pertaining to the Underworld
civitas	tribe or polity
crannog	an artificial island
crescentric	crescent-shaped
cwmwd / commote	subdivision of a *cantref*
cyfran	gavelkind inheritance, where all sons (and in some instances daughters) benefited equally
deposition	deliberate placement, usually for ritual purpose
dux bellorum	'leader of wars', a late Roman military title
epigraphy	inscribed material
fire-dog	iron hearth-guard consisting of uprights and cross-pieces
foederati	irregular mercenary troops hired by Rome
forum	the usually open, rectangular public space and market area in the centre of a Roman town
Gallia Comata	literally 'long-haired Gaul', a term used by Caesar to describe the tribes living in the heartlands of Gaul, north of the Alps
Hallstatt	label given by archaeologists (from the Austrian burial-site of that name) to the earliest Iron Age in Europe
hypocaust	underfloor heating system in Roman baths or houses
iconography	imagery of humans or animals
insulae	'islands' – the blocks of land within a Roman town
La Tène	label given by archaeologists (from the Swiss lake-shore site of that name) to the main period of the

125

	European Iron Age, particularly its distinctive decorative geometric art
lacustrine	pertaining to lakes
leaf-crown	head-dress depicted on Iron Age human images, consisting of two large, comma- or leaf-shaped designs curving inwards above the centre of the head
liminal	to do with edges and boundaries
littoral	shoreline
llan	now generally translated as church or parish, originally the enclosure of the churchyard
llys	court
mithraea	temples dedicated to the Persian god Mithras
mortarium	coarse-ware mixing-bowl
ogam	alphabetic script using lines running at different angles from a vertical base-line
oppida	urban settlements (after the term used by Caesar)
ordo	the town council which governed the *civitas*
principia	headquarters building in a Roman fort or fortress
radiocarbon dating	a scientific dating method involving the examination of the radioactive isotope C14, which remains in organic material after death. All living things take in C14 during life but cease to do so at death. Thereafter, the unstable C14 decays at a steady rate, and measurement of residual radiocarbon in flesh, wood, bone or other organic substance reveals the date of death, within a wide or narrow margin of error (standard deviation)
romanitas	assumption and display of Roman culture, romanized ways
repoussé	relief decoration on sheet metal produced by punching up the design from the inside so that it appears raised on the outer surface
schematism	stylized, undetailed way of depicting images
shape-shifting	transformation from human to animal or *vice versa*
steelyard	horizontal cross-piece for scales, used in the weighing of produce
styli	pens
tegula	flanged Roman roof-tile
tetrapylon	four-sided triumphal Roman arch or gateway
torc	tensile neck-ring, worn by Celts as a symbol of status

triplism	depiction in threes
triskele	three-armed curvilinear design
vexillation fortress	a Roman military installation that is legionary in form but smaller and, as a consequence, has been interpreted as having been occupied by a vexillation or detachment of legionary troops
vicus	civil settlement associated with a Roman fort
votive	ritual action (literally in response to a vow) involving gifts to the gods
yin-yang	La Tène design consisting of a circle divided by a spiral

Index